TIKTOK YOUR BUSINESS TO SUCCESS

YOUR ULTIMATE GUIDE TO INCREASING YOUR SALES USING TIKTOK

HERBERT KING

CONTENTS

INTRODUCTION

Sophie is not just an ordinary girl; her perfectly executed pirouettes have charmed many hearts on TikTok. Her faithful audience devoured her smile and poise and how she applied cosmetics. Before long, a famous cosmetic brand approached Sophie. For so long, celebrity models had represented the brand, but in these changing days, Sophie, a young girl in her teens and with no archetypal grooming, is on her way to becoming an internet sensation. You can change the name and put yours instead. You too can become a TikTok star if you can sing, dance, rhyme, and make people laugh with your funny and origins jokes.

A TikTok influencer with a million followers could charge $10,000 per sponsored post. An influencer with a hundred thousand followers could earn $150 per follower through daily donations to his live stream. If a thousand out of a million followers participated in the live stream, it would mean a lot of money. And most of these influencers are not beyond the age of twenty.

If you spend some time on TikTok, you may cash in on your pastime. You will get a name, fame, and money.

If you are a budding entrepreneur, there is probably no better place than the social media platform to advertise your products or services. The advertising trends have truly changed to become more people-centric.

Gone are the days of huge billboards skirting the busiest thoroughfares and highways. These were previously the only forms of advertisements, featuring the faces of supermodels smiling down at you, telling you which dress or car to buy. The mode of business advertisements was already changing with artificial intelligence and the Internet of Things and data analysis to a broader web presence; the COVID-19 pandemic made the change appreciable and faster.

The brands that, for time immemorial, stood for purity and fundamental values are now more likely to take down-to-earth approaches to reach out to the masses, and the most cost-effective and fastest route to reach out to modern consumers is through social media.

The netizens are increasingly driving commerce, and they rely on the word-of-mouth of a single individual they trust to give them an authentic opinion. They know that this individual is one of theirs, has the same tastes and interests as they have, and will only suggest to the audience to buy something if the product convinces them. Enter the influencers in the world of commerce and entertainment.

The internet and social media have plucked the street artists of the world onto the internet and given them more social outreach and commercial relevance, and the new face of marketing is the social media sites like TikTok. This is where the consumers can talk with the "brand" and talk about it globally. The netizens "hold the numbers" to decide trend movement.

You can be a part of this global picture. Whether you are a user of TikTok, an entrepreneur, or a content creator, TikTok can always provide you a means to showcase your talents, earn fame and translate your ventures into money-making profits. With 3.7 billion active users and going, it surely is a potential source of alternate income.

But to turn your efforts into a gainful undertaking, you must know how to monetize your following. It depends on a good strategy. This book explains how you can become an entrepreneur on TikTok, use its tools, and create a successful platform for value-based services or selling products.

CHAPTER 1
WHAT IS TIKTOK?

If anyone tells you that TikTok stands for Real Short Video, it would be a reductive definition of the social media site. It is much more than that. TikTok described itself as the leading destination for showcasing eye-catching short-form videos shot solely on Android or iPhones. Its mission is to inspire creativity and bring joy (TikTok, Our Mission).

The concept of short-form video making is not original to TikTok, and its predecessor, Vine, started as a short-form video hosting service in 2012. YouTube published the first short-form video lasting for 19 seconds, *Me at The Zoo*, by Jawed Karim, in 2005, and indeed many people thought TikTok was the bite-sized version of YouTube. Since 2018, when TikTok landed overseas, its progress has been unstoppable.

HOW IT STARTED

Its parent company, ByteDance, located in Beijing, China, was founded in 2012 in a four-bedroom apartment. Its first product in China, Douyin, gained popularity. In November, when ByteDance acquired Musical.ly, a Chinese short-form video-making app, its initiative was to step outside China.

Musical.ly was a short-form video streaming and sharing app with more than 100 million users; the users utilized its generous offer of music and dialogue options to create funny and entertaining videos with which they could lip-sync. Some of its content creators rose to the hall of fame; they could share the videos on other social media platforms like Instagram. This twist increased Musical.ly's popularity.

Later on, when TikTok acquired Musical.ly, it kept the video-sharing option on other platforms, and it increased TikTok's popularity as it did with Musical.ly. Indeed, TikTok gained everything with the acquisition. It received the full quota of Musical.ly's users who found their app handle changing its logo overnight. Alex Zhu, Musical.ly's founder, became TikTok's first vice-president. TikTok was always sure of its footsteps, and it never failed to make bold and decisive steps to promote the app's popularity and utility among a wide variety of users.

What is TikTok?

TikTok app has the same short-form video-making concept as Musical.ly. However, it has a wider range of applications. One can directly upload videos shot on Android or iPhones on the app. Its bouquet of sounds, music, and video templates and an option to add special effects and filters to make the videos high-quality makes it more interesting than Musical.ly.

The creators can make thousands of different video categories ranging from dance, magic tricks, song, funny facial expressions, and others. Features like filters, background musical scores, and stickers can make an amateur content creator shine like a pro. The content creators can collaborate and create split-screen duet videos when the partners share different locations. But TikTok was not to remain satisfied with this tagline for long. It was almost like it knew from the beginning what it could offer and wanted every interested party to utilize its scopes fully.

Its Popularity

Guess, the famous denim manufacturer, found its sales slumping in late 2018. It partnered with TikTok, because they correctly identified Generation Z and the Millennials as the targeted audiences, and launched a hashtag campaign, #InMyDenim challenge.

The app users could see the hashtag challenge when they were on the app. They could participate in the challenge, and all they had to do was get themselves into denim and shoot a short video that they could upload on the app (*King, 2022*).

Guess and TikTok grabbed the social media headlines. Edward Park, the SVP of Guess's retail and digital section, famously commended the youngsters, mentioning that they were the "future of social media and culture." The challenge was fun, and the denim-clad participants posted hundreds of videos appearing in all imaginable avatars.

When TikTok ventured into the international U.S. market, its contenders, Instagram and Snapchat, were the top-rated apps.

TikTok knew it had to offer something new to its users. It engaged Insta-famous persons or influencers to serve more appetizing content to the audience and provided technical assistance to make the videos high-quality. Well-known content creators eager to explore more joined TikTok. One of the content creators, @ourfire, enjoyed a fan base of 2.3 million.

Users can make an in-app purchase of coins of value from 99 cents to $99.99 in order to tip to their favorite content creators on the app.

TikTok was the most downloaded app on the iOS platform in early 2018 (*Nelson, 2018*). Its active users were more than 300 million, which reached 837 million in Q2 2020. It grossed $1.9 billion in revenue in the same year, an increase of 457 percent yearly.

Reasons Behind Success

Within two years from launch, TikTok had more than 500 million active users, with the majority located in the U.S. Americans downloaded the app more than 80 million times. In the months of the covid pandemic, when people at large stayed at home due to government sanctions, TikTok seemed to provide an avenue for distraction from the prevailing gloom and doom. In 2021, the app had 1 billion active users per month worldwide (*TikTok Statistics, 2021*).

It was available in 150 countries globally, including Russia, Thailand, and Japan. About 75 languages worldwide are used on the app.

There had to be some good reasons for such tremendous popularity. TikTok had to understand how to attract its populace.

But there are other grounds for its marketability. Several celebrities and brands joined TikTok, including Rihanna, Britney Spears, Amber Rose-Gill, Arnold Schwarzenegger, Fenty Beauty, and others. They liked and endorsed the app. TikTok professionally engaged them to drive viewership, and some, like Jimmy Fallon, started a challenge for their viewers on the app. Their attempts generated increased app downloads.

Jimmy's #Tumbleweed challenge urged the viewers to post under the hashtag videos of themselves tumbling down like a tumbleweed; he kickstarted the event by tumbling down himself. The challenge was ludicrous, and soon, everyone was having their thrill tumbling down in all possible ways. 10.4 million engagements drove over 8,000 tumblers to participate in the hashtag challenge within a week.

Celebrity partnership was a crucial factor in TikTok's expansion across the globe. They posted engaging content and interesting challenges that drive viewership, bringing their own viewers to the app site. Those who were on other social media platforms, as many were, publicized the app in those locations.

It engaged celebrities like Kinoshita Yukina, Watanabe Naomi, and others in Japan. In India, it hired Ashika Bhatia. TikTok believes in preserving the local language, culture, and tradition—all its celebrities are native to their region. It stressed using local flavors for video content, things that are relevant to the region, and tapping into local values and sentimentality.

In Japan, it came up with the "We Found My Roots Challenge," in which Japanese children got a chance to show what they received from their parents. They told the viewers about their family and themselves.

The challenge, which showcased Japan's unique concept of unity among cultural diversity, was made using the local script of Katakana. The "seaweed dance," a funny video challenge, went viral in China, with people creating a plethora of videos around this hashtag challenge (*Geyser, 2022*).

TikTok picks local buzz and fads to form contests and challenges using locally popular hashtags. Its 1 million audition contest is operational across several countries globally. The contestants, the subject matter, and the language are specific to that location in each place.

The participants get themes on which they have to make videos with the most popular video creator bagging the award. It helped generate thousands of locally made videos; for TikTok, it meant increased local presence and acceptance of the brand.

The app sends a personalized recommendation to each user as if it can read their minds, knowing exactly what they would like to see. Its users remain updated on the latest fads and always have some new things to create.

A Practical App

It is easy to create a video on TikTok. All one needs to do is choose a funny and relatable incident in their daily life, make a video, and upload it on the app. Since the video is a short clip, watching it or making one is not time-consuming.

As soon as the user opens the app, they land on its 'For You' Page. The videos created by the app's algorithm appear, and the video feed plays them one by one. The content of the videos is always eye-catching, simple, and engaging, effectively pegging the viewers to the app for hours on end.

For instance, how would you react to the meme if it reads, *"When you told your mom you'd keep the duck for 2 months but it's been 2 years."* *@yyudy.*

You don't need to follow your favorite creator; the app knows you love their work, and it will curate them just For You.

TikTok offers free applications and guidance; it wants the creator to produce their best with the potential for going viral. Tracks on TikTok are rich sources of memes, and the meme generation has created many celebrities on the app. To date, everyone remembers Lil Nas X's jam "Old Town Road." The meme caught 67 million views as it galloped, singing its way to the #1 slot on the Billboard Hot 100, and stayed put for the next 17 weeks.

Why is it Attractive to the Brands?

It seems rather strange for an app not to have a dedicated space for advertisements and yet to be so attractive to brand promotions. Unlike many other social media sites, it is not a so-called marketing channel. Its appeal among brand advertisers is for the more obvious reason: TikTok's acceptance and popularity among the young generation, who drive the style craze. Facebook, a conglomerate of apps, is the largest social media site regarding audience size and advertising revenue. However, its target audience is in the age group of 35-44, 55.6 percent of which are men.

Brands are, however, on the lookout for a target audience more youthful and ready to buy stuff without further ado. TikTok can provide that space and not Facebook. 69 percent of TikTokers are between 13 and 24, and 60 percent are women. The users spend, on average, 46 minutes a day on the app. These super-influential Gen Z determine the wave of hot topics up for discussion and the voguish style craze, be it on fashion, culinary fads and ideas, Fenty Beauty's new products, or the new wave of famous dogs. They cannot stop buzzing all day long.

Brands use the trendy hashtag challenges and content to generate content related to the brands. They also collaborate with the app's celebrity content creators to promote specific brands. A study by Adweek published that 15 percent of adults and 36 percent of GenZ purchased goods based on TikTok recommendations (*Lundstrom, 2021*). It even compiled a #TikTokMadeMeBuyIt that received more than 200 million views.

Social Media Marketing And TikTok: A Very Valuable App

The current trend of commerce, post-COVID, points to online shopping. All businesses are making a beeline to attract potential customers online. Historically, people depended on brand names, which signal quality, assurance, and guarantee to consumers. That scenario has changed a lot nowadays. Brands have contenders, some selling products much cheaper and more functional. The brands have also come out with trendy and utilitarian designs to remain afloat. The question remains one of quality.

71 percent of consumers who have a good purchasing experience with a social media brand are likely to recommend it to others. With its large number of young users and with purchasing power, TikTok is an automatic choice of brand advertisements (*D'Souza, 2021*).

With TikTok, which is used primarily on smartphones, people can watch videos on the go. A short and engaging video clip is an adroit way of capturing the viewer's attention. TikTok's interactive content is notable for its quirky, addictive quality that evokes a positive emotional response from the viewer, many of whom share a connection with the app. More and more brands are considering

TikTok for social media marketing reach, and the app doesn't seem to disappoint their aspirations.

Some Successful Marketing Campaigns

The Chipotle restaurant chain organized a Halloween "Boorito" coupon-winning campaign. The users were encouraged to dress up in costumes for the occasion and post videos on TikTok under the campaign. It was a family challenge, an initiative to launch a group ordering feature on the Chipotle app. The prize offered for five families or small groups of friends included a free food Chipotle gift card for one year along with the honor of the title of Chipotle Celeb (*TikTok vs. other social media platforms, n.d.*). It was a fun-filled contest and successfully generated four billion views.

e.l.f.Cosmetics collaborated with influencers and created an online reality show. The contest, named succinctly #eyeslipsface, got more than 3.8 billion clicks.

The NBA created an awareness-enhancing account among young people worldwide. It has 12 million followers as of February 2021 (*These Brands Will Inspire Your TikTok Strategy, 2021*).

What Are Your Chances of Standing Out?

In an app where millions of people post content, each jostling with the other to grab audience attraction, your chances of making an impression is a million-dollar question. In 2020, a video created by social-media personality Bella Poarch went viral, capturing the title of Most Liked Video. What was its recipe? No one knew for sure; it may have been due to clever camera work that captured a lip-syncing, tongue-twisting, eye-rolling, and warping funny face. The fascinated audience could only do what it must: vote it to the podium.

Bella Poarch has her designated way to stardom on TikTok; it meant around 100 million fans and million-dollar deals. Bella gets sponsorships from brands like Moncler, Google, Tinder, NYX Cosmetics, etc.

To become successful on the app is no mean challenge. You can visit the app for entertainment, you certainly will be sucked into the whirlpool of animated excitement, and if you stay for long, you will also want to create something of your own. TikTok is going to kindle that passion in you, tempting you to jump on the bandwagon.

But a word of caution. Go unprepared, and you will certainly drown in the ocean of anonymity. Bella Poarch may be performing comic faces, but there is a very calculated method in her madness. You must understand the fundamental premises of TikTok before you proceed further.

Why Was TikTok Created?

Let us revisit the time a gummy bear tugged at our hearts. TikTok appeared around the corner with the sad demise of Vine.

A lonely red gummy bear stood center-stage singing in Adele's voice "Someone Like You," when suddenly, Adele's voice cut off only to be finished by an invisible audience joining in as the camera panned over a crowd of gummy bears in a riot of colors.

This was the inspiration behind the #Haribo challenge, and anyone who has watched the gummy bear show will vouch for its simplicity, authenticity, and audio-visual appeal. It was a wholesome show that certainly did more than generate a handsome profit for the app.

That is TikTok's USP and the reason why it attracted millions of like-minded energetic people passionate about showing something new to the world. The crowd needed to be young because this generation is the most creative and explorative.

TikTok uses the power of music and eye-catching videos to tell the stories of the daily lives of ordinary men. It has its own way of telling stories and seeks to bring out the funny or entertaining side of an otherwise humdrum existence.

After all, we make funny faces and sing to the beat of foot-tapping, but converting that into profit-generating endeavors needed a lot of planning. TikTok uses a powerful algorithm that learns about your preferences so fast that it seems a little spooky.

The algorithm places the content on the For You Page, and most of the viewers spend their time here on the app. Depending on your first few activities on the app, it knows exactly what you want to see and doesn't waste time catering to your wishes. It also shows you the content that it *thinks* possesses virality; it believes that if the idea behind the content is genuine, it should go viral irrespective of the creator's number of followers.

Communities On The App

Community is the key reason behind the app's success. It is available in 155 countries and speaks 75 languages worldwide. Ninety percent of the app users visit it daily and more than once.

The app's main community-making feature is "Duet." Users can make videos coexisting with operational videos sharing a split-screen format. They can choose only the music from the original with a note of credit – "original sound" – at the bottom of the video. The app will take you to the original TikTok video if you tap on it. You will also see all the videos using the same "original song."

In no time, you, too, will start singing alongside and may wish to mime the band of musicians to make your own video and post it using the same tagline. Maybe you will hum it throughout the day, much to the chagrin of other family members. You cannot shake off the sense of belonging to a community of "original sound."

It's apparent why memes and challenges on TikTok have the potential to get viral. The technique used is simple. Any new video is shown to a small group of users. You scroll down to see the next video after you have watched the first one that appears on your For You Page.

The content gains importance in TikTok's philosophy; the creator travels behind their creation (*A Brief History of Tiktok and Its Rise To Popularity*, 2020). If the video has a good response regarding likes, comments, and shares, it pushes further ahead. After enough runs, it becomes viral.

The app is highly engaging; it keeps in mind who its users are. To satisfy the young generation's picky taste, it caters to them with variety. It has a vast music repertoire called "sounds," franchising music from brands like Sony Music, Universal Music, and Warner Music. It presents the video makers with diverse topics, including comedy, baking, grooming, food, sports, fitness, DIY crafts, etc.

The app is the new hang-around spot for the young generation across the globe, and it encourages the formation of communities depending on their shared interests and identity. You find communities like "Alt" or "Deep" that are not in the app for making money but only to form an association of compatible people (*Tidy & Galer, 2020*).

It is also a seat for action-driven youth movements like #BlackLivesMatter or the U.S. teenager's post on the plight of Uighur cotton pickers that went viral, leading to the banning of Chinese cotton fabric.

TikTok publishes only those videos that meet its approval, it is a data mining giant, and there is no doubt about that. Still, most data showed that the app's data collection amount is comparable to other social media platforms like Facebook.

Chapter Summary

- TikTok is *the* app for the younger generation.
- Its content is a short-form video (15 seconds) with songs.
- Everyone can use the app for fun, engagement with a like-minded community, and business.

In the next chapter, you will learn if and how TikTok can help your business.

CHAPTER 2
CAN TIKTOK HELP YOUR BUSINESS?

You may own a business or have a service to offer. You may be a brand owner or a brand employee; you are looking for a place to advertise your brand or services quickly and widely but also cost-effectively. If your target audience is the millennials and Gen Z, TikTok is the best option you have.

Even for older generations, a survey shows a rise in the popularity of TikTok. Their curiosity about the app is driving them to use the app. According to a June 2020 Statistica report, a third of TikTokers are under twenty, 14 percent are between 40 and 49, and more than 7 percent are over 50. Considering that there are 1 billion active monthly users, TikTok is a popular destination for advertising and marketing products and services.

GROW YOUR CLIENTELE

The platform allows you to post short-duration videos lasting 15-60 seconds, in-app editing, and collaborate with other important social media sites. The videos play on a repetitive loop.

The app provides features to enhance your video creation; you may add filters, graphics, fun effects, text, and choose a musical score from TikTok's vast music collection. TikTok also provides video formats, and some popular themes are lip-synching clips, short comedy, and popular skits.

You may increase your chance of viewership by adding trending hashtags. It makes the video more noticeable. TikTok hashtag challenges invite users to participate in major contests and themes. If you post a video in response to a hashtag challenge, you get the opportunity of showcasing your video to all the users of the hashtag. You may go viral.

What is TikTok For Business?

"Don't make ads. Make a new trend."

In 2020, TikTok introduced a new platform and brand, TikTok For Business, to announce that it was opening up for business. It was to offer all present and future marketing solutions to brands. It contains access to its ad formats.

TikTok ads are brand statements in theme, presentation, and performance. The app provides a consolidated platform offering the advertisers comprehensive guidance for ad creation, marketing strategy, setting budgets, targeting and reaching the correct population, and analyzing business data.

It means that the brand advertisers don't have to waste resources on planning marketing strategies; instead, they can concentrate on creating skillful videos that will promote viewer engagement and improve brand awareness. With the right approach, many viewers turn to customers; some of them are the repeat ones and act as brand ambassadors by sharing online the excellent experience they had with the brand.

According to the TikTok holiday guide, 74 percent of TikTokers mentioned they came to know about a product from the app, and a whopping 67 percent said they bought a product only after following an ad on the app.

TikTok acts as a guide and mentor to the brand advertisers. It even has an e-learning center teaching advertisers the content creation know-how on the Ads Manager Platform.

The only format for marketing on TikTok is an advertisement. You can leverage the app in your favor, but it's better to understand its ad formats first. Its Ads Manager platform offers five different layouts to choose from.

The Ad Formats

Top View Ads

The distinctive feature of the TikTok ad format, the Top View ad, appears once a day when the viewer opens the app. The ad can run up to 60 seconds with audio. Since the duration of the Top View ad is more than the other formats, this video format is suitable for products that need a longer duration of viewer engagement, like movie trailers.

In-Feed Ads

In-Feed ads are shorter – between 5 and 15seconds in duration, and stay on the app for only a day. These ads appear on the For You page of the user that displays content based on TikTok's algorithm. The algorithm's A.I. chooses content according to viewer tastes and interests.

Advertisers use In-Feed ads to convert viewers into potential customers by applying a strong Call To Action (CTA) to the videos to drive traffic to web pages, external landing sites, or TikTok business accounts for the brand. For instance, a health-based app can use a strong CTA to expedite the viewers in downloading its app.

TikTok advises the creators to design the ads vertically, keeping in mind to leave safe zones in the corners so that the app's user interface overlay does not obliterate the key elements of the ad.

Branded Hashtag Challenge

The app allows the user to co-create content by using the app's unique user-generated content aesthetic. Brands that use this format have preferential access to the hashtag, an advantage over other social media sites. This ad format runs for six days. The format includes a Hashtag Plus to add a shopping feature to the experience.

The ads can appear in the standard In-Feed placement, urging viewers to participate in the challenge, or on the Discover page under the featured banner. From the latter site, the traffic finally arrives at the Hashtag Challenge page, the core area where videos submitted on the challenge from around the world collect.

Brand Takeover

These expensive ads are full-screen, weighty ads the user first sees on opening the app. Usually created for mass awareness of a product, this ad assures high-impact and greater audience reach. The entire screen is clickable, and the viewer effortlessly reaches the desired ad destination.

The ads are short and kicking, either a three-second image or a three- to five-second video, landing the viewer to internal and external landing pages. The viewer sees only one of these ads per day—a 100 percent Share of Voice for the day they run.

Branded Effects

The users can add 2D, 3D, or AR effects either in the foreground or background to the images of their products.

The AR effects challenge Snapchat's Sponsored Lens and Word Lenses AR formats. You can use them for an individual campaign or a branded hashtag challenge. You may apply them cleverly to highlight a product, transforming the whole artwork into a bright and vibrant display.

Brands use various ways to spread brand awareness. For instance, they can create stickers of their products or make bespoke filters the users can use to make user-generated content videos.

Branded effects are most deftly used for CPG, retail, and entertainment ads, and to some extent by travel or automotive ads.

The Principle of TikTok Marketing

Before considering the platform as your marketing spot, you need to define your target audience. TikTok is mainly visited and endorsed by the young generation, many of them in their twenties. However, with its complement of packages like the Holiday Package, the app is increasingly used by all household members. All its users share a common characteristic: they look for direct connections. You are genuine to them, and your duty isn't over with uploading your ad video.

You have to be an active participant, engaging with your audience on the app. The more meaningfully you engage with your audience, the better the audience will receive your post. You may also take advantage of TikTok challenges, inviting users to create videos around your brand. This type of "user-generated content" builds brand reputation and attracts potential customers to your site.

Perks of TikTok

TikTok offers you the scope of gaining user-generated content. It's content that the brand's customers or followers create. They may wear, for instance, the beautiful scarf they purchased online from your e-commerce site and post a smiley face with a few exciting words about how thrilled they are to receive the item. In effect, your customers act as your brand ambassadors and do the job better than a celebrity. People look for authenticity; 55 percent of consumers trust UGC more than any other form of marketing (O'Brien, 2015).

TikTok UGCs stand out for their witty captions and short duration. TikTok knows that users provide the most authentic and cost-effective way to determine fashion trends in the current marketing scenario. Marketing for Gen Z means SINC, where S stands for short-from, I for influencers, N for native, and C for Co-created (*TikTok launches user generated content innovation for brand marketing strategy*, 2019).

Therefore, the app facilitates UGC creation, and the users gain from exposure to the official TikTok guidance for content creation.

TikTok can help you create fresh and spiffy content for your brand to drive the audience crazy. After you hold its business account, you can design a hashtag challenge around your brand. Invite the TikTokers to participate in the contest and offer the winner a prize. The audience is hungry for original, pithy, fresh, and funny posts, and if your post has all the right ingredients, it will go viral.

In-Feed ads provide links to your videos with which you can direct potential customers to your website, app store, or e-commerce store that you own.

TikTok ad formats like the Top View ad and branded takeovers have provisions for "brand recall" and "brand recognition." The Top View ad, which places your ad to the viewers who are likely to become customers, reminds them of your brand and the offers you made when the time to purchase comes. Branded takeover ads are stunning; the audience remembers the ads' emotional appeal, exceeding your aims for guaranteed impressions.

We will again analyze the Guess challenge to find out how its ad appealed to the customers.

Guess, famous for its innovative and sexy apparel, was facing a slump in its sale in late 2018. It was when TikTok stepped into the US.

Guess, and TikTok partnered, each for their mutual benefits. Guess felt the need to reach out to the young generation— the hallmark of modishness, and according to its SVP retail and digital section, Edward Park, the trendsetter of social media and culture. He considered Guess's partnership with TikTok an "exciting evolution in the digital marketing strategy."

Guess wanted to promote their Denim Fit Collection and build a new brand image, sexier, daring, and more confident. It targeted Gen Z and the millennials during the "back to school season."

The brand initiated a hashtag challenge, *#InMyDenim*, urging users to post content stating their fashion style in denim on TikTok. The challenge had to be one of its kind, and with that in mind, Guess added the slogan, "Transform your outfit from a mess to best-dressed. All you need is denim!" The concept was thus, "Transform your looks."

Guess published many brand videos with Bebe Rexha belting out, "I'm a mess." The song was a perfect fit, apt for the challenge, and fitting to TikTok's trait of exploring the fun-filled and jazzy side of a musical score.

Guess collaborated with a social media marketing agency on the first day of the challenge. They decided to launch a brand takeover campaign to increase consumer awareness. At the same time, four influencers released video clips to introduce the novelty of the concept. Together with the influencers, the Guess challenge generated 1,600 user-generated content.

The challenge was viral, earning millions of views, shares, and comments. In six days, a duration for which branded takeover ads last, the campaign reached over 5,500 user-generated videos, 10.5 million views, a 14.3 percent engagement rate, and more than 12,000 followers (*What is TikTok For Business, n.d.*).

TikTok For You

TikTok is for you if you have a business that mainly caters to the young generation and households. Whether you want to make people aware of your products or services, or wish to sell them online, you can showcase your products in an entertaining video format. All you need is the energy and inclination to engage with the app and its community.

TikTok's e-learning center under the aegis of TikTok For Business will teach you about the app and how to leverage its treasures. You come to know how to launch successful ad campaigns and use the Branded Effects Partner Program. It includes product guidance, resources, and the best practices manual to be the ultimate creative genius.

TikTok made its stance clear: It visualizes itself as a contender for the premier position in social media marketing, providing a site where brands create works that will become a part of the TikTok community and not separate entities. Indeed it prides itself in presenting maximum user-generated content following successful ad campaigns.

TikTok wants to share with you its dream of becoming a platform where cultures and trends are created and shared instantly, globally. Its motto is unity in diversity.

Like YouTube's BrandConnect, TikTok is to create a Creator Marketplace, where brands and influencers can discover each other and collaborate to produce paid brand campaigns (*Perez, 2020*).

As TikTok's MD for global business marketing, Katie Puris, mentioned, "Brands bring immense value to the user experience; we're excited to continue investing in solutions that give brands a platform to inspire others, be discovered, and meaningfully connect with the TikTok community."

If you have a business, TikTok is certainly the most likely place where it can go viral.

TikTok Can Be Important For Your Business

Social media sites are the current marketing hubs, and there is no denying it. Young or old, Asian or American, people are increasingly spending time online, surfing, chatting, and building up strong communities where recommendations are spread by word of mouth, just like in the olden days. It can be a book, a piece of jewelry, a traveling spot, or a breed of dog.

The growth of these sites both in number and proportion was only expected.

The year 2022 was preceded by a period of deadly pandemic conditions with COVID-19 that confined people to their homes for an extended time. People felt the need for human connection more acutely than ever before. The natural spin-off for global human connectivity was the social media sites, all of which took their progress up a notch. The world recovered from the scourge, as would have happened in due course, but the social media sites didn't lose their popularity or crowd.

The global market trend also altered. Marketers understood the future of business lay in the pages of websites where they could communicate with the consumers directly and get the necessary metrics for business movement.

Social media sites host community input and thrive on content-sharing and collaboration. They are used to staying in touch with friends, relatives, and family. They lessened the pain of long-distance separation from near and dear ones; people discovered each other on the sites and built up strong communities. They literally unified the world.

Businesses soon found that they could explore social media sites to promote their products and address customer concerns more efficiently. Their websites increasingly became customer friendly; they devised various tools to analyze and measure company acceptance and likeability, consumers' thoughts about the brand, and how they could better the service.

Crowdsourcing helped to form new business ideas. It was apparent that shopping shifted to social media platforms.

Why TikTok? Many joined because their children were spending time on the site. They wanted to learn about TikTok and why it attracted the young generation. Many got converted.

The Experience

Since its inception in 1997 with SixDegrees.com, the internet has witnessed a splurge of social media sites. Facebook and its family of applications still hold sway, and TikTok is a newcomer. Users are late to respond to a new member, but a look at TikTok's statistics will show how fast it became popular globally. Its innovativeness, intelligent technology, and futuristic concept have made it the ruling app of 2021 (*Daniel, 2021*).

The user's experience of TikTok is a step forward from other social media sites. With 1 billion active users buzzing on its pages every day, you may think that you or your product will get lost. It seems daunting at first, but TikTok assures you that it will be with you in your undertaking, making every attempt to see you get a top-notch experience.

Let us explore if TikTok can mean anything to your business.

The app is a social media site that allows you to create videos that can last for 3 minutes. You present your audience with music, song, dance, fun, tricks, and brilliant texts: all in one video format. If you look closely, you will find that in just 15 seconds to 3 minutes, you can connect with your audience more effectively with this format than in other types promoted by the rest of social media sites.

You may have a business account with other social media sites, but it is always better to have a presence on the site which is popular and gaining in popularity. You may create a TikTok account to reserve a spot for your business's username on the platform if, in the future, you choose to start increasing your campaign.

The advantage of TikTok is that it allows your followers inspired by your content to create their own videos around your brand. They are enthusiastic about the activity. It promotes your brand attractively and imaginatively. It will seem to you that you have a lot of collaborators with the same interest as you: your brand promotion. It is maximizing creativity using community support and participation. You will enjoy the experience.

You will be surprised to see how a genuine post can establish a deep mental connection with the audience. You may spark off user-generated content creation if your video stimulates, educates, or appeals emotionally to your fellow TikTokers.

The experience you get with TikTok is completely different from other social media sites. Shoot videos, clip them, stitch them to other original videos to enhance yours, customize audio, apply effects, and all this you can do within the app itself. Even then, the list of can-do's is not exhausted. If you are a content maker, TikTok spoils you with all the choices.

The app is programmed to listen to user feedback. If an active user likes some feature or effects, TikTok aids them by adding new editing features. It also adjusts if the active users do not like a concept.

It's spooky having an A.I. assistant recognizing what tools you want to beautify your creation and passing you just that. But TikTok does that. It is certainly a contrast to the magisterial attitude of other social media sites where users have to accept the app's dictate and not the other way around.

Make TikTok Duets And Stitch

You can co-create videos with other users and make a Duet, a video made in parallel with another video. When you post a Duet, the right-hand side of the screen shows the original video running side by side with your video on the left-hand side of the screen. It means that your video must run for the same duration as the original, adding and using the primary sound to maintain harmony.

A popular concept is the Duet Chain, where users create videos, allow others to use them as duets, and then others are invited to continue the chain. It promotes outreach of the organic content and increases the number of followers.

TikTok stitch is a tool that users can use to clip and stitch content from another user's video to their own. TikTok will credit the original creator.

An example of this can be a heart-warming UGC video you discover on TikTok related to your content. You can add it to your creation by using stitch.

Users enable stitch accounts. If you do not want others to clip and stitch your video, you may decide accordingly.

You can add features and special effects to stitch. TikTok offers a tutorial on stitch at #stitch, which has received over 19 billion views.

Stitch and duets are innovative ways to propagate an idea and forge mass movement around a theme. It constructs a creative community based on the age-old concept of remixes.

Clothing brand Mypheme discovered Roxanne Olaru hacking to create a dress similar to their own. They replied by making a video using her idea to promote the "Artemis" dress.

In their #madepossiblewithadidas challenge, Adidas posted videos, each beginning with the question, "Show me something you thought was impossible before you did it." Adidas urged users to stitch their answers as videos to the posts.

TikTokers stitched their videos doing something they thought was impossible for them to do, but they did it anyway or told stories of their achievements in response to the challenge. All of them asked the same question at the end of the videos. It created a Stitch Chain and reached more than 513,000 views.

Bring out the creative you with the TikTok community.

The Exposure

TikTok is interesting because it brings out the creative side of you. But that is not all it offers you. TikTok exposes you to a broader geographic community; its incredible algorithm makes such exposure possible. No other social media sites can provide you with the kind of audience and potential customers for your business that TikTok can. Naturally, with your consistent efforts, original content, and novel experimentations, your ability to reach millions to increase your business' potential multiplies.

For any business, the most important criteria for success are awareness by the public and exposure of your products to them. With more and better presentation, your products gain a large pool of customers, old and new, and many others who were not previously aware of their benefits may discover them on TikTok.

A video-centric mode of advertisement is more convincing than texts or images. You tell a short story through a video, and you can make it memorable.

When Should You Start?

If you are still of two minds, TikTok is not a site that will disappear like many of its predecessors. Contrarily, it is gaining momentum and strength every year and has become a serious business contender for the prime movers of social media sites. And, to match up with TikTok, many have italicized video formats to attract their users.

Recently, Instagram chief Adam Mosseri announced in 2020 that they would stress a video-centric approach to their content in the future (*Halpern, 2021*). He reportedly mentioned on his Twitter handle that TikTok was huge and posed "a really serious competition."

I would like to share an anecdote with you here. One of the big chain hospitals inaugurated a super-specialty unit in a remote area. People were doubtful of its potential.

"How can anybody access the hospital if it's located so far away?" they asked the owner.

The owner was unfazed. He said, "Once the hospital starts operating, people will automatically come when they get good service. Once they start coming, this place is going to change."

He was a visionary, hence confident in his decision. Within ten years, a whole township developed surrounding the hospital location. It became a thriving community.

TikTok has that kind of vision. It is a trendsetter. Hence, it is worthwhile to be on it if you want to market your products far and wide.

TikTok Trends

TikTok's special algorithm presents the users with trending videos to their liking. The ideas are fresh, and there is something always new. It makes content making fun and easy. Once you scan the For You page, you can see which videos are trending—they use the same kind of sound and style.

No doubt TikTok trends are compared to a live-action meme. Its videos are applicable across a wide spectrum of fields, can be easily twisted and tweaked to personal preferences, and morphed with a hint of authenticity.

Chapter Summary

- TikTok is important for your business.
- Go creative, explore, experience, and set trends with the TikTok business account.
- TikTok introduces you and your business to the global community in a unique, fun-filled way.

In the next chapter, you will learn about digital marketing on TikTok.

CHAPTER 3
DIGITAL MARKETING AND TIKTOK

Any marketing campaign involving digital communication is digital marketing. It includes email, social media, web-based advertisements, texts, and other multimedia messages.

Social media marketing is a form of digital marketing; its goals are to drive traffic and create brand awareness by establishing communication with people online. Sometimes, with some companies, the direct sale of products may not be the chief reason, and they may just want to spread awareness and interest surrounding their products and services.

Although social media marketing is an important hub for attracting B2C customers to make an emotional purchase, it has recently gained momentum with B2B customers who are more cautious and buy products based on reason and evidence. Recent data showed that 96 percent of B2C content marketers and 61 percent of B2B marketers use social media marketing advertisements (*Beets, 2018*).

BENEFITS OF DIGITAL MARKETING

Digital marketing is the most cost-effective way to reach your target audience easily and with speed. You enjoy a wide coverage with a single witty content.

There are more connections and better communications between the marketer and the customers on digital platforms than in other modes of marketing. You can collect data about your customer, making your efforts seamless and productive.

Because digital marketing immediately serves you with automated tracking of customer profiles, it can help you decide on your campaign nature. You know who is genuinely interested in your offer and gather data on related metrics.

How does that allow you to strategize your campaign? For example, you have a special offer on a life-insurance plan proposal. You can decide to split your campaign into two parts targeting the young people looking for home loans and the older generation looking for retirement benefits. Since their purposes differ, you can tailor-make your campaign into two parts to target both groups.

But how did you arrive at the customer profiles? Only digital marketing can help you to gather automated data on customer profiles with ease.

The Impact of TikTok On Digital Marketing

We all know that TikTok is primarily an entertainment site. But if one can mix business with entertainment, it turns into an exciting proposition.

TikTok has two central feeds; the For You page presents your favorite content selected by the algorithm based on your previous actions on the app, and the Following feed, where you can browse through fresh content by creators you follow. You can see content ranging from dance and music videos to branded guides and inspirational and educational content. All are in short-form video, mostly running for 15 seconds.

If you wonder at the cornucopia of video presentations, TikTok in 2021 has reached the 2 billion active users mark in late 2021, and brand marketing effectively captures this humongous number to reach all target niches on social sites.

Let us consider how TikTok can help you in digital marketing.

Building Brand Awareness

The pharmaceutical industry is difficult terrain for any marketing, including digital. Due to FDC and FTC guidelines, brands have been cautious in treading on pharmaceuticals in the social media marketplace. Mucinex, a pharma brand, took a chance when it used TikTok to promote an OTC product.

The campaign #TooSickToBeSick challenge promoted cough medicine. The theme fitted with TikTok's technical style of video-making and was called "transformation." It used *transition*, a smart editing tool that users could use to show a smooth transition from one look to another.

The users posted videos transforming themselves from "too sick" to "so sick" using the hashtag #toosicktobesick. It generated 889 million views and was a success.

TikTok is an innovative way to build brand awareness. A post on it has the potential to generate millions of views and drive viewers to your profile. By any means, this is the biggest incentive for you to compete with the latest trends and let your creativity flow.

The average engagement rate for TikTok is 18 percent in comparison to Instagram's 2 percent. 35 percent of TikTokers spent less time on TV or video content, and 41 percent have slashed down podcast listening since they discovered the app. Seventy-nine percent mentioned its content is unique or different, and many agreed that advertisements on TikTok are significantly different from other apps.

You can definitely rely on TikTok metrics to spread awareness of your business among potential customers and take advantage of educating and converting them on the app. It will be a learning experience for you and your team.

Connected Audience

Undoubtedly, youngsters prefer a platform where they can share their views, wants, and needs more than anything else. Video games, podcasts, and TV serials lack the impact of direct connectivity that social media sites can offer to their users. Each social media site has its own characteristics, and TikTok is no different.

You may not want to jump on your target audience to scare them away with a too aggressive campaign. The audience responds to visual aesthetics. With TikTok, sound, texts, and messages transform a simple ad into an audio-visual appeal.

You can capitalize on the audience's emotions to make an impulsive purchase. But the real flow of your business will depend on your long-term relationships with the clientele. You have to learn to create content that is also need-based and useful. In other words, you must understand the pulse of the audience. The trends on TikTok tell you the user's pulse. When you follow the trends, it becomes apparent to you what suits the users' moods.

Influencers who understand the needs and wants of your potential consumers are best for establishing a bond between your brand and the consumers.

You may collaborate with an influencer in your target niche. They give that quintessential personal touch to your campaign, which you may enhance by sharing a few tips and expertise to reward your viewers.

Essentially, you share knowledge and information with your audience, and the more authentic you are, the better the chances of success.

In #TooSickToBeSick, for instance, Mucinex engaged four influencers, OurFire, dreaknowsbest, Nick Tangorra, and Jaydencroes, to push the campaign forward.

The influencers bring their followers to your site, some of whom may become your customers because they trust the influencer implicitly. Such relationships between influencers and their followers are forged on TikTok.

It's Your Identity

Customers go for value. Sites like TikTok give you ample opportunity to establish your brand's story. You can use the app to narrate it in as many ways as possible.

TikTok wants you to show how you are doing things differently from others. You can show your followers how you create the content for them.

For example, if you have an apparel business, you can show how you source your material, the artisans who weave magic into the fabric, and a short snippet of your factory. You can portray your business as one big family. You can also share the highs and lows of your career path, tenacity, and faith.

TikTokers are essentially young, so do not overburden your content with a lot of ideas. Keep your posts direct and spontaneous. A video of an unrehearsed pat in the back or a hurrah in the back office can be disarmingly simple and engaging without being too overbearing.

Stories like this give authenticity to your endeavor and breathe life into an otherwise mechanical advertisement. The ad becomes your identity; your audience does not see you separately from your brand.

If you are unsure how to relate to the audience, you can engage influencers in your niche. When you collaborate with influencers who can relate to your personalities, they can help you present who you are to your followers. You may also build your identity in this way.

Your audience must recognize you. Seventy-eight percent of users mentioned that the best brands on TikTok reflect their ideas. Do you know that 53 percent of TikTokers trust those who are original (*Miller, 2022*)? They should see that you understand their needs and are interested in them, but you must be genuinely interested. The first step is to tell them who you are and what you stand for.

Arrange Training Sessions

You can use your TikTok business account to post videos on tutorials about how to use your brand. A session like this guides them and explains the utility of your products. For instance, a jewelry brand can advertise how to measure the ring size. Similarly, an apparel brand can guide users how to measure their size to make the garment a perfect fit.

As the customers go through the procedure, they inadvertently engage more with your products. What started as curiosity may turn into definitive action. The underpinning concept of all your endeavors should be entertainment, as TikTok stands for fun.

Ride On The Back Of Viral Hits

TikTok is fundamentally a lip-synching music and dance video hosting site. It found no reason to alter its persona since it is such a run-away success with the users. Even the brand advertisements have experimented with and capitalized on this concept to promote their products and fashion lines in unimaginable ways.

Use the Discovery tab to see the *trending* topics, music, and challenges, use them and experiment with them to make an avant-garde presentation. Make your audience feel that you belong to their community as you preserve the cultural bedrock and improvise it to be authentic.

44 percent of active users want funny ad content. Your video must be vibrant, fresh, and lively because TikTokers are averse to dull things.

TikTok Idiosyncrasies

We may now surmise the reasons for opening a business account on TikTok. You will reach a vast target audience, most of whom are young who spend an average of 850 minutes on the app per month. Users in the U.K spend 27.3 hours per month; in the U.S. and Canada, the figures are 25.6 hours and 22.6 hours, respectively.

Nine out of 10 TikTokers use the app more than once daily. By 2022, there have been 3 billion installations of the app, and 167 million TikTok videos have been watched in an internet minute. It received the highest social media engagement rates per post, which made TikTok a natural choice for brand presence.

According to Statista, 32.5 percent of users in the U.S. are between 10-19 years old, and 29.5 percent are between 20-29 years old. The Pew Research 2021 Survey data mentioned that 48 percent of American adults aged 18-29, 22 percent between 30-49, and 14 percent between 50-64 had used the app. The same research also mentioned that 20 percent of people with more than $75,000 in annual income had used TikTok. An older study by MarketingCharts quoted that 37 percent of American TikTokers are from households with more than $100,000 in annual income.

But TikTokers also hail from moderate to low-income groups, many of whom are students who can earn more after graduation (*Geyser, 2022*).

61 percent of American TikTokers are women, and 39 percent are men, according to a 2021 report by Statista.

Celebrities use TikTok. Justin Bieber held a TikTok Valentine's Day Livestream in February 2021. It is not a surprise because TikTokers are dedicated to music. The program was the first full-length single-artist live performance on the app, and it attracted more than 4 million "unique viewers."

43 percent of TikTok fans listen to music to express selfhood—call that teenage angst. They aspire to take part in music creation instead of remaining passive listeners. While making content for TikTokers, remember that they believe in using sounds to manifest your personality and objective, in short, your story, rather than just choosing random music from the library.

TikTok is trying its best to keep up with the spirit. Recently, it has launched a "music machine" to help you create your music from different drum beats and sounds. You should use these tools because when you use these tools, your content blends with the app requirements, and you produce a high-quality video at a low cost (*Moran, 2021*).

TikTok Power Features For Digital Marketers

Let us look at a few metrics to understand why TikTok is the best for your business' advertisements.

TikTokers love to be on the app. Sixty-four percent of users globally mention being their usual selves on TikTok. Fifty-six percent of them said they were posting only on TikTok. 59 percent of the respondents said they feel like a community on the app. Seventy percent recommend TikTok to others.

According to TikTok statistics, 46 percent of its users don't want distractions while on the site.

Seventy-seven percent of users read the comments on posts. Ninety-two percent of users respond actively after watching a video. Fifty percent of GenZ users follow the creator if they like a video.

And 67 percent said TikTok inspired them to buy a product; 37 percent said the key reason to make a purchase was an elevation of mood.

Since 2021, consumer spending on TikTok has increased by 77 percent.

In digital marketing, ROAS, or Return On Advertising Spend, is a metric that measures the effectiveness of a digital campaign. The metric helps online businesses to evaluate the efficacy of their digital marketing strategies.

TikTok advertising statistics noted that studies by many commissions found an average campaign ROAS on TikTok was twice the median campaign performance benchmark. A recent Nielsen Media Mix Model Meta-Analysis saw campaigns in the U.S. witnessed a 14 percent higher-paid ROAS on TikTok versus all digital media.

CTA in video texts provided a 152 percent lift in conversion compared to those which leave the viewers clueless. You may also want to give a product demo or sprinkle your content with comedy because it will increase the chance of viewing it to the end by 24 percent (*Miller, 2022*).

Collaborate with influencers for TikTok-specific branded content creation to avail a 24 percent more chance of ad recall. Make your content high resolution at 720p because it increases conversion by 312 percent.

In late 2020, TikTok partnered with Shopify, which soon extended to 15 countries. Shopify merchants could use TikTok business ads manager while staying on the Shopify dashboard. It was advantageous— a compact platform to plan TikTok campaigns, target consumers, and track results.

TikTok tools are flexible; you can easily use these powerful applications to make a high-class video without investing in external applications. Shopify used the app for retargeting customers and tracking ad conversions by utilizing customer data. Hashtag data retained user privacy.

Some Specific Features On TikTok

Catalog Ad

You can use a "catalog ad" format and create tailor-made content for each product. It holds crucial information about the products within the Ads Manager. You can use automated rules to shape your product specifics and make individual sets of content for each product.

Spark Ad

As the name suggests, spark ads add a spark to your content. Spark ads, launched in 2021, utilize organic social content. You can sponsor existing popular content suitable for your brand or product promotion. It is a clever quick-fix to generate awareness around your business, helping you to launch without delay. Subsequently, you can come up with your creation when you are more prepared.

Hashtag Challenge

Hashtag challenges are crowd-pullers. Hashtags are a typical form of social media interaction, and their effects last even after the challenge is officially over. Wearing a hashtag around your video makes it more integrated into the prevailing trend of social media.

However, if you want to have a successful hashtag campaign, you must be prepared with a hefty $150,000 budget plan. The hashtagged content should mention your brand's name and the stellar components of your products. You have to maintain the correct note: amusement and not pushy.

Hashtags should grab immediate attention and be easy to write. It should suggest activity; the easier, the better. Avoid unintelligible language, symbols, or numerals for a hashtag. You may avoid using a date or month in a hashtag; there should be no suggestions to show how old it is unless it indicates a celebration. Using a reference in time gives your hashtag a restricted shelf-life.

Share your challenge across all social media where you are present to maximize your returns. TikTok allows you to do that. If you are uncertain of your skills, you may collaborate with an influencer.

What Else Can You Do On Tik to Tok

TikTok's Auction Insights show graphical representations of different campaign performances and yardsticks to give your content your best shot. You can locate Auction Insights in View Data within the Campaign of the Ads Manager.

Don't be deceived by the misconception that the majority of TikToker is young, and it wouldn't be much of a help in your business. According to TikTok, its rapidly growing age demographics lie in the bracket of 25-35 years and more. The 25-34 year-old segment grew by 22-24 percent in 2021, and that of 35-plus years by 19-25 percent (*Cherepakhin, 2021*).

Why Is TikTok The Future Of Digital Marketing?

The most important reason for TikTok's success was its straightforward appeal. You didn't have to be a nerd to understand it. Its video format makes the displayed products more enticing and consumable. Indeed, when Hubspot Content Trends Survey was conducted in Q3 2017, 54 percent of consumers wanted ad formats to be in video mode than text. Soon, it became a lifestyle concept.

The TikTokers like the app because there are no impossible standards to challenge them; they just need to be spontaneous. Users use it to create native posts contributing to the heterogeneous assortment of user-generated content. Since Gen Z grew up with the internet, they use the applications for creation more proficiently.

TikTok's 15-second narrative style is innovative. The "micro-narrative" model indulges curiosity. According to the American scholar E. M. Rogers, the sheer novelty of any concept inspires an idea or practice among social groups. It spreads quickly through the use of certain channels of communication. Dubbed the "theory of diffusion of innovation," his hypothesis may explain why the short-form narrative mode of TikTok video received wide acceptance.

TikTok manipulates the user psyche; we think "big things" are the fads or crazes reported by media. TikTok utilizes this when it sets the agenda with its challenges and hot topics like finger dance and seaweed dance. It stimulated the users to post original content on the themes and interact on the app. This way, TikTok got noticed by millions of netizens (*Choudhary et al., 2020*).

TikTok skillfully guided the users to generate content on matters of common interest or actions, creating the feel of a TikTok family. Mutual acknowledgment and open communication between like-minded users improved content shareability (*Ahn, J., 2011a*).

For any social media site, the addition of celebrities is an indicator of its popularity. Justin Bieber and Jimmy Fallon were not the only ones to join TikTok. Jennifer Lopez, Will Smith, Amy Schumer, Paris

Hilton, Marshmallow, Rihanna, and many others have opened accounts with the app, and some, like Rihanna, used it for advertising their brands.

TikTok boasts of a bevy of influencers who grew up on the app. They know the app and their followers intimately and drive social media trends. You can collaborate with them to boost your ad's movement.

Remember the Chipotle campaign? Chipotle collaborated with influencers like Brittany Broski, Zach King, and JifPom to make the campaign viral. Brittany wrote in her TikTok handle, "@brittany_broski the duality of man. On Oct 31 u can get a burrito for $4 if u come in costume after 3 pm." She didn't forget to add a CTA, "EAT UP MY BABIES!!!" to the hashtag ##Boorito@Chipotle.

The gaming industry prefers TikTok to advertise its wares. One of them, EA Sports, used TikTok marketing campaigns to disseminate awareness of gaming products like FIFA 20, Apex Legends, Plant vs. Zombies, and others.

It used the assistance of influencers like Indie Cowie, Gil Croes, and Brent Rivera. Even brands like Walmart considered TikTok a fertile marketing ground to explore. It targeted the young generation on TikTok through #DealDropDance, a Black Friday Campaign.

It engaged six influencers who had a consolidated number of 17 million followers. One of the influencers, OurFire got 57K likes and 739 shares on the video of a couple dancing in a store, expressing their joy at the deal they made through the Walmart Black Friday Sale.

Other brands that used TikTok to reach out to the audience are Charlie's Angel, Kool-Aid, Gymshark, and Calvin Klein. They collaborated with TikTok influencers to promote their brands, proving that renowned brands find TikTok committed and dependable.

Influencer marketing heralded a transformation in the social media marketing scenario. Traditionally, business promotion was a serious affair and was under the domain of white-collar people.

TikTok brought a breath of fresh air into the digital marketplace by introducing a batch of fresh-faced youngsters who could sway millions of people like them with apparently extempore ideas that were hilarious and lighthearted. How could merchants ignore this potential?

TikTokers receive influencer marketing well because they share a bond with these influencers. The influencers are ordinary people, many of them very young, sharing the same outlook and inspiration as the average TikToker. It fostered trust-building that the brands could leverage to build a faithful consumer base (*Collen, 2020*).

How Can You Use It?

To get the best TikTok advertisement opportunity, you must identify your target audience, decide on the type of marketing campaign, and give it an attitude. For instance, a jewelry brand named its lightweight jewelry Me In Action. The idea was to promote "workwear" jewelry that was low-priced, fashionable, and a must-buy.

If you consider influencer marketing for your products, you must collaborate with people in your product and target niche. With their dedicated group of followers, influencers can rapidly spread product awareness. TikTok's new ad features enable one to incorporate into their video links to connect viewers directly with their online shop making it a one-stop destination for shopping.

You can have some provisions for rewarding your customers. It can be a promotional offer, a discount on the first purchase, or a free follow-up service. You may also extend a thank-you note to the influencer by offering them discounts on your products or free samples of the products.

A Few TikTok Marketing Ideas

TikTok ad formats are five in number; each is adjustable, and you can manipulate them in countless ways to suit your style. All of them appear in high-traffic areas of the app and guarantee viewership even if you are new to the app.

The In-Feed ads appear on the For You page between organic content. Use a clear CTA on your video to guide the users to your app, a website, and check out the products or your profile. Branded hashtags and Branded effects increase audience participation and engagement with your product.

Before you create something, you must know who it is for. You need to research the demographics of your target audience, like their gender, age group, ethnicity, cultural habits, geographic location, and economic condition, among others. You must have a grasp of their behavior and interests. If your work has no defined target outreach, it will likely get wasted without impacting any individual.

You should follow brands similar to yours to identify posts that receive maximum engagement. You can use the hints and create an honest version representing your idea.

Once you have identified your target audience, you can create an appropriate video like a meme. The six common video types on TikTok are videos based on popular songs, challenges, hashtags, influencer collaboration videos, and lip-synching videos.

Tutorials about baking and recipes or DIY engaged 60 percent of users. 59 percent want to know the current trend and events. Other ideas are makeup, dance moves (57 percent), product demos, workout tips, etc. You can prepare a series of content beforehand and release them sequentially to avoid errors and maintain the flow.

You must get your creation in front of the world. You have devoted time, patience, and effort, and you need the best outcomes. To get maximum viewership, you must know the best engagement time when your audience is on the app. Their geographic location matters most.

You can visit the Followers Tab and Follower Activity sections to know when and which days they are most active. TikTok records its timings in UTC.

The TikTok Business Account allows you to measure your performance metrics for one month after you have published your post. Access it to know how you did and what more the audience may ask of you (*Redhead, 2022*).

TikTok's marketing team is always there to assist you with your queries.

Chapter Summary

- TikTok is crucial in digital marketing.
- Although the app and its users are young, they are the ones that set future trends and drive commerce.
- TikTok efficiently guides you to leverage its applications.

In the next chapter, you will learn more about digital marketing and understand its scope concerning TikTok.

CHAPTER 4
A GLIMPSE AT MARKETING ON TIKTOK

Those concerned about the excess use and reliance on internet data may have had their reasons validated by the recent data published by the Pew Research Center Survey conducted from Jan. 25-Feb 8, 2021. Still, there is little evidence that the users of this mode of connection and communication are attentive to the words of caution of the wise. What did the data reveal?

Interestingly, 7 percent of Americans did not use the internet at all. Thirty-one percent of American adults have reported being almost always *online*, up from 21 percent in 2015. And if we consider 48 percent of people who are online several times a day, a whopping 85 percent of the adult population remained internet bound.

Forty-four percent of the internet consumers belonged to the age bracket of 18-49 years old. The number was higher among college students, higher-income families, and city dwellers.

We have to accept the current trend, which also indicates the burgeoning prosperity of online shopping. People are increasingly inclined to shop at ease from home comforts; most of their wants and needs are satisfied by e-commerce. Marketers know they must connect with the consumers at the place they frequent most, and at present, it is on the social media platforms.

INBOUND MARKETING OR DIGITAL MARKETING

Any form of business-related activity carried out on the internet is digital marketing, hence also referred to as online marketing. Businesses use the internet for search engines, social media connections, sending and receiving mails, offering newsletters, and directing customers to the brand websites or encouraging them to download relevant apps. Communication now is done on social media sites, through multimedia messages and texts, instead of the erstwhile telephone calls.

The tenet of digital marketing apparently differs from inbound marketing. Inbound marketing is an all-encompassing approach to business, where a marketer thinks about the goal of the business before they consider what tools they are to use to reach the customers. They then ponder which stage of the sales funnel should customer conversion occur. For all practical purposes, digital marketing and inbound marketing can co-exist to ensure the digital marketing channels work toward specific goals.

What Is Digital Marketing?

This form of marketing uses electronic devices like mobile phones, laptops, etc. Digital marketing specialists collect online data on business metrics, relevant customer information, and consumer behavior. Your transactions will remain on record for other promotional offers and sales notifications if you are a customer.

You learn about brands and businesses from advertisements shown online such as display ads, online videos, search engine marketing, paid social ads, promotional e-mails, and social media posts. In contrast, more traditional forms of advertising include billboards, newspaper and magazine ads, direct mail, and, surprisingly, television channels.

Almost all the businesses have an online presence, even the most traditional ones. It can be a website, a social media account, or a digital ad, but businesses are not taken seriously by consumers without an online footprint.

The advertisers target both B2B customers and B2C customers through digital marketing. The strategies to attract them to any business involve skill, judicious use of creativity, and experimentation with different online marketing methodologies.

B2B clients need proof of purchase functionality, and they buy things for a reason. They rely on other people's comments on the product and do market research on their own before buying it. They take time to make a decision and seldom make impulsive purchases.

B2C clients, on the other hand, make emotional purchases. B2C companies offer them "feel good" messages, which can be sophisticated style or owning a prestige brand at reasonable pricing.

Depending on who you target, your ad formats will change appreciably. For B2B, you need to provide more information. You can use video formats with a strong CTA to guide them to your website or app installation, where you need to deliver more data and research-based content on your product effectiveness.

B2C content creation is easier; you can explore social media gainfully to capture the attention of these groups of customers. They are happy with user-generated content, and you can be flexible with ad formats; however, for your ad campaign, you may need to select those which are more popular.

In many instances, the differences may blur; for example, your target audience must be wider in the automotive sector or software applications because the products are not for a specific client section only. When you need to consider both short-term and long-term businesses, you may have to select advertisement options that have a broader approach.

As a business owner, you must know how to use the free and paid channels to align your ad campaign with your marketing strategy.

Types of Digital Marketing

Some of the effective modes of online marketing are SEOs, social media marketing, email marketing, etc.

Because it involves direct audience participation, social media marketing is one of the most engaging and effective digital marketing strategies to drive brand awareness and traffic. Some of the common sites used are Linkedin, YouTube, Facebook, and Instagram.

Ninety-six percent of the marketers are predictably B2C; however, B2B companies also lean toward social media sites for brand advertisements and ad campaigns. In 2019, according to data released by the Content Marketing Institute, B2B content marketers' number on social media increased by 61 percent.

There are reasons why business people, irrespective of their customer classification, find social media sites interesting for advertisement. It is not only about a direct purchase; you may use social media sites primarily to generate awareness and take time to engage positively with your potential customers while building up a follower base. For instance, if you are a chocolatier, you can release short-form videos of your craft. You can share recipes, tips, etc. Once you gather enough popularity, you may direct your attention to sales.

How you want to avail of the social media platform for business depends on your business goals. A business may not have been your original goal at all, and you may have arrived there inspired by your fan followings. Or, conversely, it may have been your strategy to attract long-term sales instead of push-selling products.

You may choose pay-per-click (PPC) marketing when you pay for your ad whenever someone clicks on it. The PPC campaign entails the user to complete one or more target actions after clicking on an ad. These actions are called conversions. Conversions do not mean direct sales. It may involve subscribing to a newsletter or booking a spot in a webinar program. You choose what actions you require your target audience to do, and you can measure your campaign's progress on the platform.

You can also use the platforms for affiliate marketing. You earn money on commission by selling someone else's products. The key element in affiliate marketing is to find the best merchandise in profitable sectors like health, finance, and electronic gadgets and software. You get an affiliate link which is your unique tracking link for your business.

You can place the tracking link on emails, blogs, or websites, and whenever someone taps on it, they arrive at the product's landing page. If the person makes the purchase, it traces back to you, and you earn your commission.

You may affiliate with one or multiple marketers reviewing their products on blogs or a third-party site. You may associate with one for your business promotion. Whatever is your aim, you need to establish a connection with the other party. There are designated platforms for affiliation; however, you may start a program yourself or engage a participant in a program.

When you affiliate with a partner for business promotion, you should provide them with the requisite tools and promote incentives for positive impact.

Another form of advertising is native advertising, which melds with the prevailing content of the site and does not seem glaring. Many consumers criticize blatant advertisements and the content maker for having an overbearing attitude.

A "native ad," on the other hand, engages the audience through critical information or emotional appeal before it presents the products. It is because of this reason, you must use words like "sponsored," "ad," or "promoted"; otherwise, your target audience may have no clue about its intention.

When people know what they are interacting with, they are more comfortable about it and more receptive to the advertisement. It is never good to lead unsuspecting customers down the garden path, and honesty is important in business transactions.

When you use social media sites for ad campaigns, you can use marketing automation tools to improvise it. It helps you to connect more effectively with your target audience. You can gather and explore customer information to understand what appeals to them and send well-timed promotional messages to interested groups of people. It also helps you to plan focused advertising campaigns.

Many automation tools offer prospect engagement with a message about when and how the subsequent correspondence will happen. You can, therefore, make a customized marketing strategy in real-time for each of your clients without spending extra time on them.

Advantages Of Digital Marketing

Digital marketing, particularly social media marketing, is more cost-effective than traditional advertisements because, with single content creation and post, you can reach millions of users as long as it remains active.

For any form of business, advertisements drive sales and generate revenue. You want to know the number of customers your business attracted, how they came to know about you, and if they made a purchase. You may also want to know their experience with you and whether they are likely to refer your business to others. With traditional marketing, it is difficult to collect data. Digital marketing software automatically tracks and gathers information related to trading.

Data collected digitally is more accurate and well-defined. You can easily identify your target audience and categorize them for your niche products. For instance, if you are a bookseller, you can categorize your customers by their age, gender, interests, hobbies, and language. It helps you to present each with their choice of books. This type of customization is possible only with digital advertisements.

You can communicate with each potential buyer on the social media platform. You can reply collectively or individually to the shares, likes, and comments and reply to their queries. The more you attract "buzz" around your product, the greater is the "product differentiation."

Your product needs to stand out from the rest of its kind. It helps build and fosters brand loyalty (Amadeo, n.d.). It means that you take pains to explain the benefits of your product, and it satisfies the needs and wants of a target audience.

Digital marketing provides for fast conversions. After seeing an inspirational or attractive ad on a social media site, users often purchase. Sometimes a customer may "save" items for future buying, thus moving down the sales funnel.

You get a chance to interact with them to remind them softly about the products they wish to buy. Therefore, you are neither ignorant nor too presumptuous in your approach to the consumer, and only social media marketing can allow you to foster such a one-on-one relationship with your customers.

Why Has Digital Marketing Become So Important?

When most potential customers spend a large chunk of their time online, digital marketing seems sensible for product and service advertisements. The Pew Research Center released a mobile fact sheet on April 7, 2021, which noted that 85 percent of Americans own a smartphone, up from 35 percent found upon the first survey conducted by the same institute in 2011. 94 percent of Americans between 18-49 years of age own a smartphone, and 15 percent of American adults access the internet only through smartphones.

Digital marketing enables you to access many people for your business. Your product reaches the consumers instantly whenever they use social media platforms or other forms of digital engagements.

Modern customers endorse digital experience; they love doing product research and making informed purchases, which necessitates any marketer to use different forms of digital marketing. Social media marketing brings your product to prominence, while you use Google search engines like SEOs for product information. It means that you need to think of setting up an interconnected network of platforms for effective product display, available research materials, and information regarding product details. The consumer must be able to see your company's work when they search online for more information.

However, it is not the only way a customer makes an informed choice. Blue Nile Research performed a market study in 2015, "The Content That Compels People To Buy," with about 528 Americans. The study revealed that 79-82 percent of consumers use search engines, brand websites, and customer reviews to make purchase decisions; social media share of all site visits increases based on organic content. The same study showed that a considerable percentage of the population used social media sites, blog posts, and website information for buying things.

The study was small-scale and old; the trend toward digital marketing has escalated. The ensuing pandemic, physical restrictions, and the considerable ease with which consumers could gather information, select products, and purchase made this mode of purchasing journey preferable over others.

Unlike traditional marketing, the speed with which you can reach your audience, interact with them, create leads, and convert leads to clients is possible only with digital marketing. It helps build a trusted customer base at a reduced cost of advertisement. For instance, according to Blue Fountain Media, the cost per impression in print (CPM) is $1.09, unlike that of digital ad, where the CPM is $0.01078 (*Sherman, 2019*).

With traditional marketing, your ad may not reach the right consumers. When you choose the right time to place a video ad content based on your target audience demographic, you can hardly miss them from interacting with your content.

You can easily update your content or customize it on digital platforms, seek ideas, and perform market research which is never possible in traditional advertisements. You can offer exclusive pricing options apart from discounts or special sales. You can measure campaign progress and conversions with ease. If you wish to collaborate with others or engage professionals like the influencers to generate leads, digital marketing is your place to be. Undoubtedly, this form of marketing gives you a better return on investment (ROI) than traditional marketing, which it may not replace, but can complement.

Your competitors are on the digital marketing platform, creating new followers, generating leads who may turn into a client, engaging with users, and motivating decision-making. When you join digital marketing, you participate in the happenings of world marketing trends which, as predicted by three prominent global ad agencies, the Magna, Zenith, and GroupM, will exceed $300 in the U.S. ad market and $700 in the world in 2022 (*Adgate, 2021*).

Modern brands use both free and paid digital marketing strategies for better outreach. Search engine optimization (SEM) is the best-paid option for B2B and B2C marketers; search, and social media ads are the most popular destinations for marketers to interact with consumers (Hysi, 2019).

Consider how we all gather information— through digital media, it should be why you need to take your business online if you are not there already.

TikTok As A Digital Marketing Agent

Can TikTok satisfy all the requirements and privileges of digital marketing advertisement? The answer to this question is affirmative; it can and in a fun-filled, engaging way. What can be a better choice for a marketer?

Many brands discovered TikTok by serendipity. Ocean Spray sales and Fleetwood Mac streams zoomed in 2020 following Nathan Apodaca revving up the #DreamsChallenge by riding to work on a skateboard when his car broke down fortuitously on Sept. 25.

Nathan, unfazed by his predicament, drank cran-raspberry juice (Ocean Spray) and lip-synced to the lyrics of the classic jam "Dreams" by Fleetwood Mac as he skateboarded, capturing his morning adventure on TikTok. Inspired by his "morning vibe," the viewers commended the trend-setter by grabbing cans of Ocean Spray to make their versions of the zen culture video and uploading them on TikTok.

The event got so much momentum that Fleetwood Mac cofounder Mick Fleetwood joined TikTok and posted his version of the popular video on Oct. 1. Fleetwood Mac, which was founded in 1967, made a sales turnaround by 374 percent and an 89 percent jump in streaming. Their hit music was once again on Billboard's top chart.

Ocean Spray provided Nathan with a new truck to commute to his workplace.

Let us explore how TikTok can help with your brand advertisements.

TikTok advertisements increase brand awareness, create an interested community, and help product sales and services. You can use the site to get customer feedback and offer them helpful suggestions or guidance. You get to know your target audience, making your ad campaign more differentiated and robust.

Brands leverage TikTok for three broadly different types of marketing.

TikTok Influencer Marketing

Like Nathan Apodaca, TikTok became the host to many other content creators who could deftly turn a challenging situation into an enjoyable moment. They showed the world the wonders of kinesics. Their viewers were too happy to imitate them, and they creatively generated videos on the organic posts to drive successful trends.

TikTok still retains its original flavor, and unlike its competitive sites, TikTok doesn't have a professional air. Its spontaneity is what TikTokers love about TikTok. Since the influencers are native to TikTok, they can feel its pulse to create heart-warming content.

TikTok created superstars of Charli D'Amelio, Addison Rae, and Zach King. They were our boys and girls who rode on public craze to become household names. They have millions of followers who flock to them wherever they are. However, you do not need a big name to generate leads for your business. A micro-influencer with more dedicated fan-following is better suitable for the purpose. They give better ROI, as they have genuine followers who trust them, and they have deep insights into the audience's psyche, helping them produce more believable content.

You must select an influencer who fits your product's or service's purpose. It would help your business when the influencers belong to the same geographic location as your target audience; for example, if you own a cosmetics brand in Ohio, you may want to engage an influencer who belongs to that particular sector and lives in America.

You can create an influencer yourself. For example, you may request one of your brand followers with a good number of fan-following to market your brand. In return for their service, they can earn rewards for themselves and their families or friends with a gift voucher of your brand.

You can take the help of an "influencer grid" to look up an individual in your area. This tool gives you detailed information on the influencers, like their number of followers and views or shares of their videos. You know their native countries, and if they are suitable for your product advertisement.

Become An Ad Creator

If you want to make an ad, you need to create a business TikTok Account for your brand. You can enjoy the freedom to create your own ad; after all, who else can better understand the value of your product and services? On TikTok, truly, the possibilities you have at your disposal are endless.

Use your talents to showcase your products, make day-in-the-life videos, create dance challenges, and urge users to participate in hashtag magical transformations. You will enjoy your sales journey as the customers will enjoy their purchasing ones.

TikTok Advertising

If you can invest money into advertising your brand, TikTok is the proper palace to start. Many brands owe their success stories to the strategic brand advertisements on TikTok, like Aerie, Little Caesars, and Maybelline (*Hirose, 2021*).

There are five ad formats on the TikTok for Business: In-Feed ads, Brand Takeovers, TopViews, Branded Hashtag Challenges, and Branded Effects. These are typically costlier than competitive brands like Facebook, the minimum cost being $500.

In-Feed ads blend with TikTok content, with one exception: you can add multiple CTAs to the video format linking them to your website, app store, product page, or for other actions. The purpose of the CTA is for viewers to arrive at the destination you want them to.

In-Feed ads can be creative; with varied skillful motion graphics, you can narrate a complete story using your imagination artistically.

Brand Takeover ads are very costly, but you can reach millions of users with a single ad that runs for one day.

TopView ads are unique forms of In-Feed ads; the users see these ads first within three seconds of starting the app. They appear at the top of the For You page, can be up to 60 seconds duration, and run full-screen. Hence, TopView ads are noticeable and, if catchy, memorable.

Branded Hashtag Challenges are probably the best for creating brand awareness. They can produce a great number of user-generated content, which can run for a considerable length of time, often after the end of the original challenge duration.

Branded Hashtags appear on the Discover page on TikTok. When users click on the hashtag, they arrive at the brand's landing page providing information on the challenge, including the website links and UGC of the TikTokers who already contributed (*Chafer, 2022*).

They are fun and are one of the most effective ways to build brand awareness and usefulness because of loads of content generated highlighting these factors. Your brand becomes intimate with the audience.

Branded Hashtags run for six days and cost a whopping fee of $150,000 for the entire duration.

Branded effects are costly, with a price tag of $100,000 per effect, but they encourage audience participation and hence, are effective. TikTok allows you to take a page from Snapchat's playbook and make AR overlays that you can use on your video. You can share your content on other social media platforms to pull an audience, but it's not just a matter of copy and pasting. You must keep in mind the unique style of TikTok. It's challenging to generate views on TikTok without engaging audio and visual videos.

Most users of TikTok watch it for small humorous clips encircled around a groovy tune, preferably with gyrating movements of the performer.

It means TikTok is an informal platform, a theme you must remember when making content for the site.

The concept that your post must get so many followers before it acquires virality encumbers many social media sites but not TikTok. On it, even a new content creator with no fan following has an opportunity of becoming famous with their maiden post. An example of this is the popularity bubba_ice got after uploading only a few videos of his ice cream jigs. His account boasted 1.3 million followers, and his videos got 21.6 million likes.

The trick is plain to sight; you need to pick a trending pattern of songs and hashtags ruling TikTok pages currently. Ride on them to instant fame. However, remember, trends change overnight; therefore, you must be able to select the right one at the right time. For instance, you should not post on a hashtag Christmas challenge in June.

You can also create your hashtag challenge and ask users to participate creatively in it.

TikTok allows affiliate marketing; you can publish videos on TikTok to earn money by directing the audience through the affiliate links in your videos. TikTok doesn't impose a curb on how much traffic you get, which is the app's most favorable advantage.

Some examples of affiliate marketing on TikTok are Grace, aka Littlemama, with 457.5K followers and 7.3 million likes. She earns through a category of deals that include Amazon and affiliate commodities. She does it by redirecting her TikTok followers to her YouTube profile.

With 1.3 million followers and 24.9 million likes on TikTok, Rachel Meaders earns from affiliate marketing with Amazon by making short videos of "things you didn't know you needed off Amazon." She uses LinkTr.ee to guide users to action.

If you have an affiliate marketing business, you can use TikTok for its huge fan base for free to guide them to your affiliate products. However, you cannot add affiliate links directly to your content. You need a "bridge" or a "landing page" for your audience to access your link. @graceakalittlemama, for instance, adds a "watch vids on YouTube" tagline replete with emojis on her content.

TikTok is for the innovation of ideas. Its plus points are how you can use its intelligent algorithm to drive traffic and engage its vast number of curious users ready to jump on the bandwagon to set the trends in a new direction.

Chapter Summary

- Digital marketing, including social media marketing, is trade and commerce's future.
- Whether you own a business or work with one, you should use social media sites for brand awareness.
- TikTok, with its huge follower base, is an attractive proposition for brand advertisements.

In the next chapter, I will discuss some brands that use TikTok for advertisements.

CHAPTER 5
BRANDS THAT USED TIKTOK'S DIGITAL MARKETING LIKE PROS

"Creative without strategy is called 'art.' Creative with strategy is called 'advertising.'"

JEF I. RICHARDS

Why are social media sites frequented by ad-makers? The key reason is they are accessible to everyone. People enjoy relative freedom of expressing themselves on social media sites leaving behind an indelible footprint of behavior patterns and activities that experts in different fields use for further studies and analysis. People in business are no exception.

Businesses follow consumer activities and demands on social media sites. It makes them aware of the identity of their target audience, what they prefer, what they ignore, and the things they reject.

Social media sites give them opportunities to understand the whimsicality of consumer behavior, search for the latest advancements in their respective fields, and get the hang of competitor strategies to help express their products or brands strategically and creatively.

HOW DO BRANDS UTILIZE SOCIAL MEDIA SITES?

Social media advertisement is the fastest, most fruitful, and inexpensive way for brands and businesses to "humanize" ad campaigns because these avenues are always open for interaction between brands and consumers. Consumers want brands that reflect their personality and day-to-day living; they don't feel close to the dissimulating celebrities atop billboards. Realizing the current demand, brands advertise on social media sites to show their genuineness.

And why not? With the number of active social media users standing at 4.2 billion globally, the netizens form a force to reckon with.

Brands use social sites like TikTok for brand promotion and sales, build consumer trust and awareness, project themselves as thought leaders, and create a presence in the most congested traffic worldwide.

Brands That Learned the Importance of TikTok

TikTok is gaining popularity among brand advertisers because of a few crucial factors.

One, it is hugely popular. Apptopia obtained information and analyzed it from Google Play and iOS App Store and prepared a global list of the most downloaded apps in 2021. TikTok topped the chart with 656 million downloads, far ahead of Instagram (545 million), WhatsApp (395 million), Snapchat (327 million), Messenger (268 million), and Spotify (203 million).

TikTok users are young and decide on fashion trends. They have the energy and enthusiasm to generate valuable UGC content. They influence and actuate the virality of content.

Globally video format is gaining popularity as a mode of communication. Interaction happens in the form of viewer likes, comments, and shares. TikTok's short-form funny video content draws immediate attention, making it the choice for quick interaction. TikTok is a global app with distinct local flavors indigenous to each country where it operates. The brands can make ads specific to the local market.

TikTok has enabled many ordinary boys and girls to achieve name and fame. These influencers are native to the site. Many of them are from smaller cities with close-knit relationships with their followers. Brands engage these "micro-influencers" for the authenticity and trustworthiness they tend to generate among their followers. Together, the merchants with their resources and the micro-influencers with their talents can make history.

Chipotle: Fast Food Chain: A History

The American fast-food chain Chipotle was the first one of its kind to have an official TikTok account. Its CMO, Chris Brandt, "ventured into the uncharted territory" because one needed to be where most of its customer base was.

Brandt's decision was flawless in timing and choice of place for advertising its Cinco De Mayo free delivery special. The challenge, #ChipotleLidFlip was put in motion on TikTok in May 2019. The challenge launched with influencer David Dobrik got 104 million views within a week and produced 110,000 UGC videos for submission.

Chipotle followed it with #GuacDance, on 'National Avocado Day' to promote free guacamole delivery online through the app. The participants in the challenge created content of their dance moves played against Dr. Jean's Guacamole song. Brent Rivera and Loren Grey of YouTube fame partnered with TikTok to create a challenge that received 250,000 video entries and 430 million views in a week. Never was a recipe for avocado guacamole this popular before.

The NBA: Athletics

The NBA is devoted to TikTok advertisements. Digiday stated that the NBA had a team of employees wholeheartedly focused on posting an assorted number of videos on different themes daily on

TikTok. It released inspirational videos of how athletes kept themselves fit even in quarantine during the current covid pandemic.

The NBA TikTok account has something for everyone; it spreads awareness about athletics among the audience through light-hearted entertainment. Its VP of social and digital content, Bob Carney, was all praises for TikTok that helped them "cultivate the next generation of fans."

Gymshark: Fitness Niche

Gymshark is a fitness apparel and accessories brand prevalent among fitness enthusiasts; it was on Instagram and had 2.9 million followers. Gymshark decided to seize the attention of a young demographic. It delved deep into their aspiration to come up with a new-year motivational challenge. In 2019, it chose TikTok to reach out to 2 million TikTokers, had an engagement rate of 11.11 percent, and #gymshark received 45.5 million views.

Gymshark collaborated with six influencers in the fitness niche who had more presence on TikTok than on other social media sites like Instagram. In January 2019, the brand launched 66 Days: Change Your Life Challenge, one of its most successful ad campaigns.

Gymshark has always cleverly chosen themes that go well with its brand: workout videos, challenges, and motivational fitness stories (*Goodman, 2020*). Gymshark videos show the athletes are just about to perform some undoable feats; the viewers watch breathlessly, and just when they are eager for more, the video stops. It's an audio-visual masterstroke, and Gymshark followers love watching it.

The Washington Post: Newspaper Giant

The newspaper keeps its approximately 1 million followers happily engaged on TikTok; the symbol of The Washington Post's TikTok account, Dave Jorgenson, is the "TikTok Guy." He has 1.2 million followers, and his videos received 51.3 million likes to date.

Amazon: Online Retail Store

"Things TikTok Made Me Buy," "Things You Didn't Know You Needed Off Of Amazon," and the likes are testament to how much Amazon depends on TikTok users for sales promotion. It may not sponsor or draft the video scripts, many of which are through affiliate partnerships with influencers, trusting them to produce original and engaging content.

Mountain Dew: Soft-drinks Niche

Mountain Dew engaged wrestler and actor John Cena to promote its new melon flavor soft drink in early 2021 (*Reitere, 2021*).

The soft drink advertisement on TikTok invited TikTokers to count how many Mountain Dew Major Melon bottles people could see flying in the air. Each contestant could make three guesses; Ryan Depaul grabbed the prize with his first guess. Cena announced that the first correct guess would receive 100,000 in prize money.

In 2020, Mountain Dew, a brand of Pepsico, promoted its new "sugar-free" soda water drink with a Super Bowl campaign released on Instagram, Snapchat, and TikTok. It got its campaign ideas from Stanley Kubrick's "The Shining." In the challenge, TikTokers used a branded effect to superimpose themselves on the supernatural twin girls from the movie in a clip from the brand's commercial presenting the new drink. The users had to use a hashtag, "BetterThanTheOG," attached to the brand (*How Mountain Dew, Hyundai and Chipotle are weaving TikTok Into Super Bowl, 2020*).

Mountain Dew astutely manipulated TikTok's special effects that acted as a mirror, duplicating a mirror image of the content creator. Eric Chin, Mountain Dew's senior marketing director, mentioned that they were the first CPG brand to create ads using an effect on TikTok.

They were very thorough with their campaign; knowing that TikTok videos prefer dance themes, Mountain Dew engaged a choreographer to work alongside TikTok in creating one of the most watchable ads.

The Story Of Gymshark: A Case Study On Influencer Marketing Strategy

Why should you go by blogs, articles, or posts that promise to give valuable marketing tips? When you Google search marketing strategies, the search engine obliges you within the blink of an eye with countless websites on the topic. It is challenging to glean correct information from a load of traffic, some outdated, some controversial, and others confusing and unhelpful.

When you are about to invest precious resources like time, money, and energy in a project, you have the right to know the authentic information—the inside story of a particular brand's association and journey on a platform.

A case study provides an exhaustive account of a company's specific tools and strategies to weave success stories and the lines of action they had taken to that effect. A case study highlights measurable results like engagements, awareness generated, rise in popularity, sales, and profit.

There are different ways to perform case studies. One of the methods is to explain the company's tactics and how they affected its growth. They are relatable and show others the effective way to do things through setting examples. They offer "proof" that certain strategies work.

Brands thought the same about social media advertising. It was a strategy that would work. 90 percent of consumers were on the internet to explore a local business, and 82 percent read reviews online (*Pitman, 2022*).

I have, therefore, presented two valuable case studies to show how and why famous brands leveraged TikTok, relied on its applications, and benefited from its favorable atmosphere. Their stories are "social proofs" that an advertising strategy on TikTok is valuable for your business.

TikTok achieved its popularity among a generation of young people central to business proliferation, both production, and sales. This generation, the GenZ, used TikTok extensively to showcase themselves: their ideas and creativity around an idea.

TikTok, which promoted its content in short-looped musical and dance performances, was amply suitable for the youngsters to present their shows to the world. TikTok spread fast to 150 countries adopting to retain the local flavors wherever it went.

The pandemic may have hastened its rapid growth. However, it would be unkind to pin everything on the pandemic. TikTok's super-intelligent algorithm had a lot to do with making utterly novice boys and girls famous with their lively quirkiness. TikTok provided them a platform where they could be original and thrive being so.

Many of them became influencers on the platform. As influencers, they set trends, drove conversation around a hot topic, inspired users with educational and personal journeys, and promoted constructive use of a powerful tool for communication.

The bond between the influencer and their followers did not go unnoticed by the brands. Many of them were already into digital marketing and used social media sites for brand awareness and one-on-one communication with the consumers.

Brands traditionally engaged celebrities for brand promotion and sales. It was perhaps the time to change their strategy. They realized that people trusted the influencer because they were from the same background and better understood the audience's sentiments than the celebrities.

TikTok's success stories in creating indigenous influencers with big fan bases soon impressed the famous brands. Some of the brands were wise to target the young generation who flocked to the new platform around the corner. TikTok, the influencers, and the brands formed a triad that took the advertising world by storm.

Gymshark, Influencers, And TikTok

UK-based apparel business Gymshark, founded in 2012, was not much older than its business marketing partner TikTok. It was the era of android based social marketing. In the summer of 2018, Gymshark's sales reached 52.8 million, and it ascribed much of its success to its influencer marketing strategy.

It worked alongside the Instagram influencers right from the very beginning. By the time the company decided to hop onto TikTok, it already had a 2.9 million fan base on Instagram.

The company chose TikTok to promote its fitness apparel among the young sports enthusiasts partnering with influencers in the fitness and lifestyle niche.

It launched the "66 Days | Change Your Life" challenge on January 1, 2019—the day of making new resolutions for the upcoming year. The *goal* was to spread brand awareness among the audience, but Gymshark intended to forge a unique and dynamic bond with the participants.

It engaged influencers in the respective areas with more fan bases on TikTok than other social media sites. It believed TikTok native celebrities could forge a more meaningful connection with their followers.

Wilking Sisters had at that time 1.1 million fans. Gymshark selected them. Others were the Rybka twins with 5.2 million followers, Laurie Elle with 2.5 million followers, and Twin Melody with 6.3 million fans. Lesotwins and Antonie Lokhorst were the others, with 1.2 million and 3.5 million supporters.

Some of the influencers shared their Gymshark posts on Instagram. The action directly supported Gymshark's business interests, but it also helped TikTok. More people came to know where things were happening. If anything, sharing content on a rival platform increased TikTok's brand awareness.

TikTok videos are mostly dance and music sequels, and Gymshark didn't want to upset the well-accepted format. The influencers performed choreographed dance movements to set music. Twin performance is another acknowledged concept on TikTok, and four of the influencer account operators were siblings. They posted varied content related to dance movements, gymnastics, and lip-synching activities.

The videos were made in a 15-second format, and they urged the users to choose one of the individual goals they wanted to accomplish and work towards it. The contest opened on January 1 and ended March 8, 2019.

The participants needed to post videos of themselves before starting the challenge and 66 days after they wind it up. They uploaded the videos linked with the designated hashtag on TikTok, each having a fair chance to win the prize: a year's worth of Gymshark products.

The challenge consisted of nine types of activities per week; the first week was #ActiveEverday66, in which the user could walk to the office instead of driving or take short work-out breaks during office hours.

The subsequent challenges were making meaningful changes in routine, educating oneself about something new, working in small ways toward a healthier self, making positive changes that matter to the world, etc.

The challenges occurred during the pandemic months, and Gymshark made its eighth-week challenge, #Mindfulness66, one of participating in mindfulness activities. The ninth-week challenge, #Supportlocal66, went big on the importance of local things, like local businesses, tourist places of attraction, and local service utilization.

The users could participate in one, a few, or all of the challenges, but they had to show progress in their journey using the hashtags every week (*How Gymshark gained 3.4 million TikTok followers, 2022*).

19.8 million users comprised the target audience; at the end of the challenge, the ads received 1,916,400 likes with an overall engagement rate of 11.11 percent, there were 12,576 comments, and #gymshark66 got 45.5 million views.

The Chartbusters

The sisters Miranda and Melanie Wilking wore Gymshark apparel and lip-synched to the hit tune, "My Boyfriend's Back," as they danced for TikTok fans. In their videos, the sisters spoke of their fascination for the paired Gymshark outfits they wore. They linked their videos with @gymshark and #gymshark66, which got 222,800 hearts and generated 1,707 comments. The engagement rate of their content was an enviable 20.41 percent.

Aitana and Paula Etxeberria, together known as Twin Melody, were successful on platforms like Instagram, YouTube, and TikTok. In their videos tagged with @gymshark and #gymshark66, the Etxeberria sisters sported Gymshark summer clothing for a stark winter backdrop knocking heart-shaped snowballs at a snail's pace. The duo told their followers how much they loved their Gymshark outfits.

The sisters had a combined 6.3 million fans who gave them 438,600 hearts. There were 3,634 comments on their videos, with an engagement rate of 7.02 percent. They also shared the video on Instagram, which received 430,133 views.

Antonie Lokhorst, a Dutch fitness influencer, had 3.5 million followers on TikTok. He performed in TikTok duet dance composition with co-worker Ramón Vermaas. Antonie's followers on TikTok loved his graceful acrobatics. Gymshark selected him for their ad campaign.

The influencer prepared a duet with Ramón Vermaas, where they did the #stairshuffle challenge and effortless airwalks on the pull-up bar. Lokhurst's subsequent posts endorsed the brand forging a long-lasting connection with Gymshark on TikTok (*Gymshark Influencer Marketing Case Study, 2018*).

Let us review the conclusions of the case study of how Gymshark planned its marketing strategies using the talents of influencers and applications of TikTok.

Its founder Ben Francis conceived the idea when he was a 19-year-old student. He didn't have any big initial plans, and it was more like, "I really want to wear this, so I made it." He chose product pricing arbitrarily.

How did he become the Forbes 30 under 30 with a personal net worth of $10 million with such an unremarkable start? At the end of 2012, Francis attended BodyPower Expo, a leading exposition on the fitness market. He and his friends put in much effort to showcase the Luxe fitted tracksuit and shelled out every penny to make the presentation worthy. It helped him to build a brand name.

After the trade show, Francis and his collaborators went online with their products. Success was immediate; in half an hour, Gymshark sold more than it ever did before, approximately $42,000 a day as against $400 per day previously.

Gymshark always focused on social media sites to create consumer awareness of their brand and products. The company owner believed in harnessing the potential of community mentality to further its aim. Many other businesses may not have agreed with their strategy, but this was Gymshark's crucial reason behind its success.

Francis collaborated with some talented social influencers and made brand ambassadors out of them. It chooses its influencers with care; they must tally with the product concept and should be able to convince their followers why the brand is a must-have for everyone.

Those who are selected should know how to present the brand attractively. The audience must be impressed by the presentation and remember Gymshark.

The influencers planned "meet-ups" before an event, where they interacted with their followers and fans to tell them how impatiently they expected to see their fans soon and how much it meant to them. It was an ethical code for the influencers to organize these meet-ups.

Gymshark chose TikTok for its popularity and the catchy concept of short-form video narrative against dance movements and music. It engaged six TikTok influencers, each famous in their own turf. The influencers collaborated with TikTok to make a motley of high-quality 15-second videos, tagging the Gymshark hashtag.

While on the challenge, the company posts published consistently over 40 content per month because it builds brand awareness. The TikTok algorithm responds favorably to consistent posts pushing them more to the users.

The brand is ubiquitous across social media sites. People recognize it for its swanky yet comfortable outfits. They would love to see themselves in one of Gymshark's apparel and the people they know and love—the influencers vouch for their adoration for the brand. What more could certify brand value?

Gymshark talks with its customers and tells them what it does and how it does them. Its Blackout FAQ page reads, "suffice to say, we rarely have sales." It added, "But when we have, we make a BIG one." It is this honest communication that builds a brand reputation.

Online social media sites are the only place where you can form a rock-solid alliance with your customers. Gymshark manipulated social media sites to suit its business purpose, like building up mass euphoria (Fear Of Missing Out: FOMO) by using a timer to strike the last few seconds to the beginning of the blackout site on the apps.

It is always innovative to find numerous ways to engage with the audience online and offline. Gymshark Central publishes articles on fashion, technique, and guidance, giving useful inputs on health and fitness, and the customers learn what they should buy (Lavendaire, 2021).

Gymshark intentionally created its identity as a health and fitness brand. At present, its market value stands at more than £300 million.

Chipotle TikTok Success: A Combination of Crowd, Brand And Music

A mere look at the climb in the rise of users on TikTok from 0 in 2013 to 524 million in 2018 which exceeded that of Tumblr, Twitter, LinkedIn, Snapchat, and others, showed why brands could not ignore the app. The only social media sites larger than TikTok were Facebook, YouTube, and Instagram.

TikTok was apart from these sites because most of its users were young. Chipotle CMO, Chris Brandt, used the term "disruptive" to describe the nature of the first food chain; perhaps it was why he chose to partner with TikTok in 2018 to "celebrate" the union of the unique forte of the two brands.

"We wanted to have a conversation with our customers and be a part of their culture and be relevant," he said. Probably Brandt was trumped by a Chipotle employee, Daniel Vasquez's 'lid flip stunt.'

When I watched the short video clip, I must agree that his performance jarred me. What had just happened? I was asking myself as much as Daniel was.

The clip got 127 910 views and may have inspired Brandt to take his brand to the vibrant crowd of TikTok. The #ChipotleLidFlip challenge engaged the influencer David Dobrik; it received 318 million views.

Chipotle signed with TikTok to promote the #Guacdance challenge, which was TikTok's highest-rated challenge show to date, getting more than 1 billion views. Chipotle also got its "biggest guacamole day," when it sold 800,000 servings in a day. On July 3st, the National Avocado Day, Chipotle's avocado use hiked by 68 percent.

Brandt credited the success to TikTok's uniqueness of dance and music video format and the timely song by Dr. Jean's Guac Dance. Loren Gray was the influencer for the #GuacDance.

His advice to others was to get a solid idea, begin small and work from there (*Kelso, 2019*). He didn't mind failures—they were learning processes for success, but with Tiktok, he never had a chance to fail. The gross expenditure of Chipotle for TikTok marketing was approximately $150 million—about 3 percent of sales. Accordingly, its TikTok budget was "low six figures."

On TikTok, Chipotle creates brand awareness through three methods. It regularly sponsors *branded hashtag challenges* and ties them around a special event, like National Avocado Day.

It is aware that TikTok challenges are short-lived and must begin at the right time and place. It jumped on the trending TikTok Tortilla Trend and the Miley Cyrus Challenge.

Chipotle utilizes *smash-hit TikTok sounds* to give character to their challenges. They select sounds with care to harmonize their product marketing strategies. In a Super Bowl challenge, Chipotle engaged Justin Bieber to invite users to sing to his "Yummy" while making ads on "February Free Delivery Sundays."

The company selects appropriate influencers well-versed in their respective field of performance. Loren Gray was suitable for the avocado challenge because she was a famous dance video specialist. She was one of the original influencers of Musical.ly, with which ByteDance merged to create TikTok (*How Chipotle Became The Most Followed Food Brand On TikTok, 2021*).

The Washington Post And TikTok Marketing: Publishers In Two Minds

The Press-Gazette published basic information on TikTok's relevance to the publishers. Accordingly, TikTok, a video-based social media app, is very popular among GenZ. It costs them nothing to be on the app. Approximately 1,000 U.S. publishers and a couple of hundreds in the U.K. and across Europe used the app to interact with the public.

The famous publications on it are The Washington Post, USA Today, BBC, NBC News, Buzzfeed, Mail Online, Sun, Channel 4 News, Cosmopolitan, and the New York Post.

The article noted TikTok was a good option to target new audiences by letting them appreciate the entertainment face of journalism. The cons mentioned were the time required to create high-quality videos and the difficulty of presenting grim storytelling in a funny video format.

Of course, the Washington Post guy, Dave Jorgenson, thought otherwise when he said, "To get people interested in politics, sometimes you have to get them to laugh a little bit."

Dave has nearly 900,000 followers and more than 35 million likes on the Post's page for TikTok. He is a full-time worker on the page and makes about two videos per day.

He chooses big news events and makes cutting-edge posts on them. Many of them do not lead the audience directly to an article in the newspaper. Why then is The Washington Post on TikTok?

The newspaper aims to produce awareness of the newspaper among GenZ, a general appreciation of the importance of journalism in day-to-day life, and increase subscriptions for newsletters and the newspaper by providing links to the content on the account's biography.

Jorgenson noted that TikTok was always forthcoming with answers to his queries on the app's usage (*Turvill, 2021*).

However, many other newspapers are still not sure of TikTok investment of resources. The platform's lack of ways to directly lead the users to publisher websites is a concern they expressed. TikTok maintained that publishers need to become skilled in making short-form videos on journalism to thrive on a futuristic platform like Tiktok.

Chapter Summary

- Digital marketing is the future of trade.
- TikTok is attractive to many brands that target Gen Z.
- The formulas for success on TikTok are right topic selection, right influencer marketing, and the right selection of song and dance sequences.

In the next chapter, we will analyze why TikTok is also for small businesses.

CHAPTER 6
ARE YOU A SMALL BUSINESS?
TIKTOK IS HERE FOR YOU

Most of us who own a business are not big brands or franchises. Lovingly called the 'Mom-and-Pop' stores, these small businesses were the backbone of local culture and tradition. They included drug stores, groceries, and general stores owned by local families. They knew everyone around and were the refuge in case of any emergency.

MODERN MOM-AND-POP STORES

Nowadays, small businesses can be restaurants, bookstores, car repair shops, wine shops, etc. They have the distinct disadvantage of competing against big names to survive. However, during the pandemic years, the renewed slogan of "go local, use local, and shop small" has made many appreciate the importance of small businesses in the economy.

What is Small Business?

What makes a business small? Is it the size of the business operation? One factor is obvious. Small businesses do not have as much capital, resources, or workforce as big corporations. Consequently, their production in terms of products or services is smaller. The U.S. Small Business Administration defines 'small' as a business that makes $1 million to over $40 million as revenues (gross income) or employs 100-1500 workers. These statistics help understand the firm's contribution to the overall market growth in terms of sales and how statisticians can use them to give better results.

For instance, the 'Limited-Service Restaurant' segment with a cut-off of fewer than 250 workers is a better choice to be considered a small business than five workers. In the former instance, the small business classification criterion made up 51.7 percent of the total revenue of all firms in the particular service sector.

However, if we consider five workers as the cut-off point for small businesses, it would amount to a mere 4 percent of the total sales in the Limited-Service Restaurant sector, although by number, it would make up 23.7 percent of all the firms. To anyone, it would seem a business full of loss.

Different metrics are used for various industries. For example, in the case of the Truck Transportation business, the revenue earned is used as a cut-off point to describe a small business.

Businesses are small when they operate out of a limited number of locations. There are criteria for that too. For instance, in the case of real estate, 1,524 firms out of 106,579 firms had more than one establishment for business, but they made approximately 50 percent of the revenue share in the industry for 2017.

In general, small businesses employ a small number of people at any particular location. The 2018 County Business pattern Survey noted in 2018, more than 50 percent of businesses had fewer than five employees. But they created 5.5 percent of employment in all business sectors. The large companies employed more people and meant more to the economy.

To make matters even, we may consider small businesses as establishments that engage fewer than 25 people; when seen this way, they employ less than 25 percent of the workforce, a better prospect than the previous scenario.

It is somewhat of a headache to determine the scale of a business. One had to make sure that they created employment, served people, and produced profits that mattered to the overall economy. While for the US Convenience Stores, standard small businesses employing less than five people supported 33.4 percent of all sales in the sector in 2017, the same criterion for Computer and Electronic product manufacturing sector in the same year accounted for 1.2 percent of the revenue. For the latter, a one that employs more than 250 workers meant 67.7 percent of shipments.

Let us look at the Ambulatory Health Care Services industry. In this case, we consider data on revenue generated as the indicator for business size. Likewise, a business with less than $5 million in revenue per year is a small business.

Businesses are also classified based on their legal structures. A corporation is a big enterprise, whereas sole ownership or small partnerships are small. The "C-Corps" businesses have a different tax bracket than the "S-Corps" who don't pay the federal income taxes.

The structure of a small business differs from a big corporation. They usually have a single owner or a small number of partners who control the business management. They are labor-intensive as they cannot afford to invest a lot in technology, and they depend on local resources, natural products and waste less. Because of their nature, they are more flexible than big businesses and can adapt to changes.

Whatever we try to define the magnitude of small businesses, they undoubtedly constitute a sizable section of the US economy and are key to its native market growth (*Hait, 2021*).

Small scale businesses can operate from small-scale industry sectors to export-oriented markets. Women own many; some are micro-businesses, village-based cottage industries, or small co-operative firms (*Meaning nature And Types Of Small Business, n.d.*).

Small Businesses And Local Economies - Why You Matter

Small businesses are part of the community feeling—a sense of giving back services to the neighborhood in exchange for a token of love and appreciation. Small businesses create an aura of belonging, of the community, by the community, and for the community.

Can you imagine your neighborhood without the pretty bakery or the friendly pet shop? The tarot card reader has her bell ringing for your attention. She gives a patient ear in your distress and offers suggestions she thinks are helpful. At the least, she distracts you from your sad mood.

Have you seen the number of people who hang around these local shops? Scientists have proclaimed the benefits of human connection, these local shops and pubs give us a spot to interact with people we know, and it makes us feel safe. You meet your neighbors and friends you grew up with at the local pub to share a timely chat. You feel good when you return home.

These businesses provide small-scale local employment, and many of us have learned the tricks of trade and craftsmanship from working there.

Indeed, they are great places to earn extra money when you are in high school. They give you exposure to customer handling, mastering front-office skills, managing cash, and key features of product display. However, small-scale businesses are more than this. Pineapple Payments (before its merger with Fiserv) described small-scale businesses employing up to 500 people.

The Small Business Administration (SBA) acknowledged the fact when it mentioned the existence of 31.7 million small businesses in the U.S. They made up 99.7 percent of firms with salaried workers. In that case, most American businesses are small, including restaurants and real estate agents.

The Bureau of Economic Development noted that the small business sector created 10.5 million net new jobs against 5.6 million new jobs created by the big companies. It has a considerable magnitude in creating job opportunities, as well as supporting many ancillary businesses related to supply chain and manufacturing. 47.1 percent of private-sector workers work in these businesses contributing to 43.5 percent of the GDP in 2019.

Small businesses applied for more patent filings, more than 16 times per employee than large patenting houses.

According to Chron reports, a community is emotionally attached to the local small businesses. They were right in their assumptions; during the covid pandemic, the local shopkeepers and businesses came to the aid of the community. Small businesses extended service to helpless and hapless neighborhoods in a diverse way, and many of them functioned at all odd hours.

What did we not get from them? Medicines, supplies, groceries, essential items like milk, and even running errands or calling emergency services for help. Suddenly, our neighborhoods transformed into a microcosm of the bigger world in the aftermath of an unprecedented event. It rekindled our faith in trusting small and local. The picture was the same in the big cities and remote villages and towns with a handful of populations. People felt a kinship with small businesses.

Small businesses were thriving even before the pandemic, thanks to increases in global consumerism. They were flexible enough to compete with the big wigs of business and came up with innovativeness to attract more and more people. Indeed, many people who lost their jobs with the big companies took to small-scale ventures to support themselves and their families. What was marginal became more relevant to the economy.

The social media sites helped small businesses advertise their products and services. The users of these sites came to know about shops and facilities in their neighborhood, often marveling at the godsend assistance.

People are reluctant to travel far or import things if they get quality goods at a reasonable price locally. And, with online service and a proper supply and delivery chain, many are prepared to pay for value.

Small business tie-ups with social media sites reach a larger audience rapidly. Increased consumer awareness leading to positive engagement and sales means increased employment for the local youth population who are out of a job or are searching for part-time work.

Small business partners often work with related small businesses to offer goods or services, creating an interdependent chain of business. It produces an ecosystem that is symbiotic and supportive of one another.

The owners of small businesses are more caring about their customers and are more eager to step out of their ways to assist. My dressmaker does not think twice about coming to my house to take measurements. She makes the dresses and takes the pain to deliver them to me. Does it sound a bit old-world? If it does, I would say we can all do with some old-world charm and grace. Not everything about business has to be about money and transactions. Human connection is more important than anything else. Big business houses are aware of it, and they try myriad ways to impress people.

Small businesses don't have that liability. Customer satisfaction comes more naturally to them, and customers think they are important to the business. We call it a personalization of service when the customer's feelings are substantiated and validated to give a tailor-made experience for each one of them.

It starts with remembering the customer's name, what their children prefer, and their favorite color; and can include many minor details that matter to the customers. A small business owner remembers all these details precisely (*Why are small businesses important for the economy*, 2021).

While the global outlook for business is crucial for the survival of many economies and trade, the local businesses give the customers a rare touch of personal feeling. Small businesses don't siphon off money to some remote offshore localities. They cushion the nation and her people against major economic changes in the market.

Before we move on to the next section, let us look back upon the contribution of small-scale businesses to our people (*Advantages of Small Business and the Economy*, 2021).

- Women own 36 percent of small businesses.
- Veterans own 9 percent of small businesses.
- People of color own 14.6 percent of small businesses,
- Women-owned businesses have jumped by 114 percent over the last 20 years.

Digital Marketing And Small Business

When you are opening a small business, what you want most is customer footfall. You are confident of your product value or your services, but you are unsure how to make others know of them. You make random choices of spreading awareness among people. It may mean distributing flyers and leaflets, engaging canvassers, or in some instances, through the print media.

You know one thing for sure: you must advertise what you are selling. The advertisement brings awareness. When people know your business, they can pay attention to what you are offering to sell. They have the scope to determine if your services satisfy their requirements. When you can satisfy their queries sufficiently, you make sales.

Advertisement helps a business grow. But you must reach the audience who matters to your sales. The language of advertising and its style should also grab immediate attention. Ads keep you connected to your audience, helping you build a long-lasting relationship that is important for making a loyal customer pool.

You may be a small business now, but it does not mean that you may not dream big. Everyone wants to grow, and you are no exception.

When you start small, take baby steps but focus on targeting the global marketing economy. If you are wondering whether it is possible, digital advertising can get your product advertisements to a broader section of the community with ease and efficiency. And, if you believe in the policy of letting customers come to you, your company's digital presence is certainly a way to help them find the direction of your business.

You can efficiently deal with a global audience by using the digital platform. Digital platforms enable you to keep track of your performance, customer pool, data on their preferences, and more. You can interact with associates, partners, and consumers on the platform and through emails and subscriptions. You can be with the customers without an unnecessarily overbearing attitude, guiding them and offering choice throughout their shopping journeys.

All information regarding customer activity and behavior, your sales and profit, and your team's effort management are available with a few clicks. You can remotely connect with other business associates and establish strong partnerships. You can even track your competitor's performances. With your laptop or P.C. and the digital platforms, you can explore endless possibilities. Some will succeed, some may fail, but all will be learning experiences that you might enjoy.

Small business owners erroneously think that their businesses are not worth going for digital advertising. They often take things at their own pace, waiting for the next move to happen automatically. They prefer to stick to a few traditional advertising methods for their business, believing their business will spread by word of mouth, and clients will bring more clients.

The thing is, clients can also take your clients to another competitor. Other businesses are eager to lure potential customers, and all are not scrupulous. Indeed in business, an aggressive promotion strategy for an excellent commodity or a valued market service makes the difference between success and acceptance of failure.

Tools like Semrush or Ahrefs can help you perform some online research on your competitor's business endeavors. Semrush is a tool for providing services like SEO, PPC, SMM, keyword ranking, competitive research, content marketing, marketing insights, campaign management, and keyword traffic to a page. You can use it to improve visibility.

You may use Ahrefs to find out your competitor's most of the linked content; Moz is another tool to find out the keyword ranking of a company. BuzzSumo tracks popular content and influencers. Google Alerts is a tool employed to track a competitor you want to research. Ontolo is a tool for backlinks and content marketing (*Why Digital Marketing is Important for Small Business, 2021*).

According to Statista, 4.95 billion people — 62.5 percent of the global population used the internet in January 2022. Of this number, 4.62 billion used social media platforms, sometimes multiple times a day. Internet use was maximum in Denmark, with the US occupying the twenty-second position in the list with 92 percent internet use.

Modern consumers like to make informed choices. Before making a purchase, they prefer to search for product information online. This is true across all marketing sectors. Even if you buy a bar of chocolate, you would want to browse sites for brands, pricing, flavors, and offers. Things are easy to search for with smartphones and the internet, and looking them up has almost become a national obsession.

Customers expect you as a business owner to have an online presence, a website, or a social media account. 78 percent of consumers use the internet more than once a week when they need information about a local business. 21 percent use the net for this purpose every day.

People would like to see the reviews of your products and whether they should invest in purchasing with you. Data shows that 98 percent of customers read online reviews for local businesses. Not only that, 80 percent would be "likely" or "highly likely" to give a review if their firsthand negative interaction turned into a very positive one (*Pitman, 2022*).

Maybe the time to say goodbye to traditional advertisement is on the horizon; maybe soon, all customers will want to know their purchase details and hold a company liable for misinformation.

Whatever it is, the future of business transactions will unfold on the digital platforms where you will acquire first-hand knowledge of consumers' online behavior as an owner of a business. Businesses will no longer function on guess work but rock-solid research into customer requirements and the prevailing market conditions.

TikTok For Small Businesses

Which brand's advertiser would not like to be on a platform that boasts of more than one billion monthly active users? After all, advertising is for making known the presence of a brand or a business. Do you know the root of the verb *"advertise"*? According to the Oxford languages Dictionary, the English word advert derives from Latin *"advertere"*: turn towards. The idea was to "turn one's attention to," which morphed into "bring to someone's attention."

Hence, you must advertise if you intend to bring your small business to everyone's attention. The best place would be where most people are. Most other brands are doing it, including small businesses. Even many who are not directly advertising on TikTok give the platform a trial.

Some people find the TikTok advertising theme alien. Still, once they start with a bit of help from the app itself (and from books such as this one), they will marvel at the contemporary approach to showcase their business to a buzzing community of the current generation.

You may still have some trepidation. You may be unsure whether TikTok can really help you to expand your business or consume time and resources. TikTok aids in business expansion. Its algorithm ensures that everyone has a fair chance to get 'good views' on

TikTok's page. Even when you are a newcomer with no followers on the app, you have the possibility of getting viral on your maiden venture on TikTok.

The For You page of TikTok is an endless flow of content, blending in a good number of videos by people you do not follow. However, the algorithm believes that you may like them anyway and share or comment positively if you want more of them. The content gets the required "push" to circulate further ahead.

What content is liked by the TikTok audience? The app wants its users to be on it, and it constantly shows the audience new content to keep them engaged. When you frequent the For You page for a few days, you can quickly recognize the pattern of things the audience prefers, loves, and shares (Strapagiel, 2021).

The product's discoverability is the beauty of the app. Many brands take advantage of TikTok's method of showing the viewers content according to their preferences rather than the posts from their "friends." For instance, when you post an ad on beauty products, TikTok will present your content to those who love watching beauty brands. You benefit from substantial social exposure with minimum resources spent.

The TikTok business account is unpaid. You can place your website on your profile when you have an account. TikTok's Linkpop page helps you arrange and categorize your products, your online store, and other types of content with a link. The customers can arrive directly at your online store if they like your content.

There are plenty of other ways by which you can reap profits from a simple business account on TikTok. Allow me to present Azure Fit, an "athleisure" clothing brand and a small-scale venture owned by Toronto-based entrepreneur Erin Dubs. She started in 2018 with tank tops but very soon, she was producing an entire wardrobe of comfortable and stylish loungewear.

Erin is a TikTok expert. She has 126,000 followers on the platform in her account @erindubs. She maintains that TikTok gives you an edge in business that you cannot ignore. There are at least 300 people on the app constantly; it can fetch you around 60,000 views in a few days.

She fondly reminisces about the first time her content went viral on TikTok. She exhausted her stock that day.

She insists that a smaller number of views can also make an appreciable difference in spreading brand awareness and the sale of products. The number of potential customers who arrive at your business's website is still desirable. If you display your products aesthetically and professionally, the visitors will remember them even when they don't make an initial purchase.

It would remind you to make content consistently on TikTok. When we see something interesting regularly, we get piqued by it. We may land up purchasing it.

Consumers purchase when struck by the innovativeness or beauty of a product. They are pampered when entertained by a person who does not have the bearings of a salesperson. Erin recounts how she struggled initially on TikTok with her concept of traditional advertising.

Erin spent two years at @AzurFit, where she exhibited her products and posted some behind-the-scenes scenarios. She found that her audience was watching but not purchasing. She discarded the account and left TikTok.

After a while, she rejoined the app, and this time she opened an account using her name. She showed her audience the natural person she was and participated in challenges. She got followers, and one day inspired by a fellow TikToker, she started posting her business on TikTok.

Soon, she learned she must be genuine in her content. She could approach her audience better if she portrayed her feelings about comfort and stylish wear—what she felt she wanted most for herself. She guided and inspired people in choosing the right kind of product. She gained an appreciable number of followers, enjoyed hosting multiple viral contents on the app, and sold her products well.

TikTok's audience believed her when it understood that she was not trying to bully her customers into buying her products.

The audience wants to get aroused by the advertisement and not get scared away. In other words, customers should get the vibe that you genuinely understand their needs; you have used the products yourself and liked them.

"It was really cool," she said. "I wasn't talking directly about my product. I was giving business tips, and that was turning into sales."

Erin wasn't the only one to share her enthusiasm about the app. Meet Bruce Graybill, creator of Sider's Woodcrafting, who was considering shutting his business when his video went viral on TikTok. Bruce said they increased traffic to their website by 4000 percent by that single viral video. His experience reflected Erin's.

Bruce sold everything they displayed on their website in a single day following the viral video.

TikTok is not a passive platform; it *wants* you to succeed, and it participates earnestly with your app ventures. Its head of Small And Medium Business Account Management (SMB) in North America, Danielle Johnson, and his team are developing more educational content for small and medium-sized businesses on TikTok.

Bruce Graybill participated in an educational show for SMB, where he recounted his story of how he got $30,000 in sales from the app alone. He advised the content creators to be on the app to make a positive difference in sales. He stressed making original posts, mentioning that what worked for him may not apply to another person (*Monllos*, 2022).

Duane Brown of Take Some Risk, a performance marketing agency, advises small and medium businesses to be on TikTok. However, he wanted you to have a paid ads revenue source like a website, blog, or affiliate marketing on Google or Facebook as a safety net.

Hacks And Tips For Small Businesses

If brands say they don't know how to advertise on TikTok, the latter retorts back, "Don't make ads, make TikToks." It states that one should not open an account with TikTok for business to do business only—that would be taking it verbatim; TikTok wants you to go creative to design ads that persuade the buyers to say #TikTokMadeMeBuyIt. As Katie Puris, TikTok's global business marketing head remarked, TikTok ads should be such that people would say, "I didn't even realize that was an ad!"

So how do you get started on TikTok?

You have to open an account with TikTok and follow a few videos. It will help you understand who TikTokers are and how the platform operates. Next, you can create a TikTok business account for your business and follow popular hashtags and a few TikTokers accounts. You should leave your opinions in the form of likes, dislikes, or comments on the videos you watch. Your actions on the platform will drive specific content to your For You Page. It will be helpful if they are of interest to your business.

TikTok has idiosyncrasies, and its language is one of those. FYP, for instance, means the For You Page. If you wonder why a multitude of videos bear the hashtag #foryourpage, it is the page you see as soon as you open the app, and it has all the trending content on TikTok (*Widen, n.d.*).

Make a few videos, and try to be natural. You may have already seen that many videos on the app are ridiculous, but Tiktok content is light-hearted, and you don't shy at letting your hair down.

Before you record a video, a few tips can be relevant. If you want to change camera direction when recording a video, just tap on FLIP on the top right corner of the camera screen, it will change its focus either to the front or to the back as per your need.

There are different speed options. You can adjust speed by tapping on SPEED in the top right corner. When you tap on the + sign at the bottom of the screen, you can choose video length to stop recording automatically after 15 seconds or 30 seconds.

To start recording, you tap on the red button, tap on it again to stop, and then tap on the checkmark.

Tap on ADJUST CLIPS on the top right corner. You may slide the red bar left or to the right to set the length of time required for the video. If you select a sound before you record or upload the video, the sound length will fix the video length.

TikTokers love recreating a theme. They select a trend and improvise on it. If you come across a trending challenge, you can join it to add your version of it. Indeed this is the essence of TikTok creation, but you must add your side of the story. You should follow the community guidelines on TikTok to adhere to the rules.

It is time-saving and intelligent to make batches of videos before you post on TikTok. TikTok will try to present your content to as many viewers as possible, but the action lasts for a single day. Public memory is short. When an app is deluged by new content every day, it is wise to post regularly. When you make many videos and save them as drafts on TikTok, you can post them one after another consistently to create an impression on the users.

Anything that grabs attention works with TikTok. Encourage your audience by urging them to make their videos. You may ask them a question they can answer or a sincere validation of your service; they can drop a hint or suggest some tricks; the more you engage with your audience, the better the outcome for your business. You can even make suspenseful mini-episodes of your brand's story.

Ordinary people make TikTok videos on their smartphones or iPhones. You should shoot them in good lighting. High-quality videos get better views, but TikTokers want originality. You can win them with original content without being too fussy about perfection.

You should add a song to your content because that is how TikTokers like them.

TikTok has a vast archive of songs and music, and they are available to you for free. If you like any song when you watch TikTok videos, click on the song name to add it to your favorites; when you do that, you can access it easily in the future for your content (*Widen, n.d.*).

You may add a hashtag to your content to make it more discoverable. The hashtags must be relevant and trending. They should not be more than three to five in number. Some of the favorite hashtags for small businesses are #smallbusiness, #businesschallenge, #supportme, and others.

Chapter Summary

- Small businesses form the backbone of the US economy.
- Digital platforms are best for advertising your small business.
- TikTok brings your business to the fore.

In the next chapter, we will understand the relevance of hashtags on TikTok.

CHAPTER 7
THE HASHTAG GAME

There are plenty of memes on hashtags, one of which asks if "#" means "pound." Another one shows an old lady peering into her ultramodern gadget (a laptop), trying to make sense of social media codes, and getting baffled by "Why Does Everyone Keep Putting Tic-Tac-Toe Thingys In Front Of Everything?" Try to guess why indeed?

For a person familiar with hashtags, their misuse may seem annoying. But a person who dons them indiscreetly around their posts in social media parlance is amateurish. If you use a platform for a professional purpose like advertising, you must know about using hashtags correctly.

"IS THAT TWO WORDS?"

Hash and tag or hashtag? And what does it stand for?

A hashtag on social media gives a feeling of community to the users. The earliest one on record was by Chris Messina made on 23rd August 2007, at 12.25 pm. on Twitter. He asked fellow users how they felt about using a pound sign for groups. He cited an example of his idea: #barcamp [msg].

Messina's coworker at that time, Stowe Boyd, named the symbol #: hashtag. He wrote in his blog that since he felt that tags on Twitter and other places talked about shared experiences of a kind one can enjoy the exposure either by actively using a 'hash tag' to the tweet or more passively by following the tweets related to a tagged topic (*Know Your Hashtag History*, 2016).

What Is A Hashtag?

A hashtag is a symbol that stands for many things: the sign of a pound, the 'sharp' notes of a musical notation, and a tic-tac-toe board. This symbol started on social media on Twitter, but eventually, its presence became a permanent and prominent feature across all social media platforms.

A hashtag is a word or a keyword phrase with a hash symbol # attached to the prefix concerning social media sites. When anyone is searching for the keyword or the hashtag, your hashtagged content gets a view.

The ease of using hashtags for content has prompted every user of social media sites to dabble with them. You just have to place the sign # in front of a word or phrase you wish to make famous.

There are a few rules to follow. You must not use spaces between the words, numbers, or phrases; there should be no punctuation and special characters. Capitalizing the words is not essential and is done only for legibility.

The symbol # can be anywhere in your post or content—beginning, middle, or the end. The social media network indexes your content, enabling it to be seen by people who are not your friends or followers.

You use hashtags for reasons. They are fads that indicate the current buzz around a topic. You must remember that social media sites are virtual communities where people assemble to meet friends, make new connections, and exchange ideas on shared interests.

The easiest way to identify a topic for discussion is to put a sign in front of a few words. When many people use the same hashtags, the subject is hot for a chat.

Hashtags streamline searching efforts; brands use them to make content or challenge reachable to a vast number of people. One of the reasons business advertisements use them is when they hope for active communication with users. Users look for popular hashtags to access posts on issues they want to discuss and participate in, which means hashtags drive action.

Hashtags get transported and utilized, and they evolve in their journey. If you locate a specific hashtag suitable for your content, you may use it to get your content across to a broader community using the same hashtag. Research by Buddy Media mentioned that hashtag tweets got twice the engagement rate than those that did not have one. Clever use of hashtags makes your content prominent and attractive to users.

When you research a topic, look for specific hashtags to get more authentic content suitable for use. Some endure the test of time, never losing their relevance. One such, #Eventprofs, is an ongoing hashtag for event organizers.

Researching the popular hashtag campaigns will help you to understand the reasons behind their success. You will know what you should do and what you should not do.

You will notice that most of the successful ad campaigns were not overly promotional, and most of them tagged the brand's name, like #Nike, #Adidaslove, etc.

Hashtags can express your personality, the fun side, or your notoriety. It may attract an audience towards you or may scare them away. Hence, be informed about what you are using for your content on social sites.

DiGiorno pizza hopped on a hashtag in 2014, #WhyIStayed.

It was a mistake they dearly paid for. Users coined the hashtag to discuss domestic abuse, and social media users were frustrated and disappointed by the insensitivity of the pizza brand.

Hashtags are like spices to your social media content; use them appropriately and in moderation to make your content noticeable (*Brooks, n.d.*). Are they useful? Most definitely. In information-crammed digital platforms, hashtags are sieves that sift the relevant.

What then are good hashtags? They must be appropriate for your purpose. A hashtag should help you reach your target audience and directly connect with your business. Just as when you write, you choose words that accurately convey your thoughts and ideas to readers, when you use hashtags, you want to make an advertisement popular. You should select those in your niche yet catchy and can relay your business's objectives to consumers.

A good hashtag must be short. Avoid those that are dubious or cunning. Use them on posts that are likely to spark interaction rather than on every post.

Hashtags can be general or specific. Specific hashtags are more action-oriented. You should give the hashtag a trial period to know if it's working. If it doesn't draw people to your site, you may consider removing it. Do not use too many hashtags; they clutter the content.

How would you know which hashtags are suitable for small businesses? You can search social media sites. Find out replies to your content, if they carry any hashtags; check accounts of big business organizations to find out what hashtags they are using for their social media advertisements and posts. Sometimes when you look up commonly used industry terms, you can land up with a good hashtag like #industrialchic, #industrialinterior, #industrialwedding, etc.

Another good option is to search for the hashtags used by popular influencers in your business category. Too obscure or too general hashtags never reach the audience.

You may use tools like BuzzSumo to find out the right influencers; you can also find content, blog articles, and publications related to your type of business. An influencer tracker tool indicates the influencers' activities, the social sites they use, and their relevance to your brand category. Other research tools for identifying appropriate hashtags are Rite Tag, Hashtagify.me, and Keyhole. Hashtagify.me reveals popular hashtags; Keyhole is a free tool with which you can track your accounts and gauge the social media performance of your competitors.

Using social listening tools like Hootsuite, Social Mention, and Google Alerts is constructive. You remain alert to communications occurring with your and your competitor's brands or products and services.

You can check all your social media accounts with a social listening tool, and if you have multiple accounts, monitoring them becomes more manageable. It is critical to be mindful of the fringe areas of your business in today's market scenario, where most of your customers are chatting unbeknownst to you about your business.

How do you use a hashtag on TikTok?

Users on TikTok apply hashtags to label their content. They are "clickable," which means you can see all other relevant content using the same hashtag.

TikTok advises you to use hashtags; they help TikTok's algorithm place your content before interested viewers. You have a limit of 100 characters, and you are encouraged to experiment with trending hashtags on TikTok. It is good to remember that the popularity of a TikTok hashtag can be short-lived. It would not help you latch onto an outdated or irrelevant hashtag (*O'Brien, 2022*). You must follow the app's Discover page to note what hashtags are trending.

Hashtags And Digital Marketing

Hashtags can be an essential tool for digital marketing, and business houses are increasingly becoming aware of their power to drive the craze. However, there are distinct strategies to use hashtags correctly in advertisements or content.

When you wrap your content with a hashtag, it gets categorized, hence easier to identify. For instance, if you advertise makeup products, using #makeup or #beauty will simplify a viewer's search for makeup products.

As soon as you use the symbol# before the keywords, the platform assigns a tag to your content, and apps like TikTok can push more specific content to a target group of users. It initiates you to a community, and the hashtag is your ticket to the fold.

On certain platforms like Twitter and TikTok, hashtags are vital to creating a follower base, particularly general content like travel. For instance, if you upload a video of your trip to the beach, using a #beach can drive your post to those interested in travel and use the same hashtag. You may sport your brand's swimwear, which may grab viewers' attention. You can even promote your brand logo using a general hashtag like #creative (*Valvano, 2019*).

However, the objective of hashtags on social media platforms is to invite people to join a discussion. You can participate in the discussion, follow it, or even research it for your company's benefit. When you use brand-specific hashtags, you miss the chance to allow people to generate conversation around your hashtag. Also, if you use too specific hashtags unrelated to TikTok's nature, your content may get ignored.

Nowadays, we hear a lot about hashtag marketing, linking businesses, brands, and people on social media sites by using the symbol #. Hashtags work with most social media sites like Twitter, Pinterest, Facebook, and TikTok, and they are galore with stories of brands who reached their pinnacle of success with serendipitous hashtags.

In 2007, Twitter started using hashtags to select the content that got viewed more. Before long, brands realized the power of hashtags, even the more general ones like #moneyblog. If the topic was relevant, people were too ready to jump into the conversation.

Hashtag campaigns set sail for victory when Barack Obama, in his presidential campaign in 2008, got a boost by the #yeswecan on Twitter. People shared it more than 3000 times. His Twitter and Facebook accounts didn't use the hashtag, but the campaign was pushed forward by his supporters, who used it many times.

Audi, in 2011, was the first company to launch a television advertisement using a hashtag. It was an experimental effort by the car company, and like all exploratory journeys, it rode on the back of the Super Bowl.

Viewers were urged to use the #Progressls and the URL audi.us/progressls to participate in the challenge. A trip to Sonoma, California, and a chance to test-drive AudiR8 were offered the winner's prize.

The campaign was popular and produced many mimicking campaigns on #WantAnR8. Audi learned that creating a hashtag challenge for social media sites made it easy for the contestants to locate the challenge and go through the content entry process without difficulty; it was also easy for Audi to comb through the contestants' content.

Even though hashtags started on Twitter, it was Facebook that, in 2013, made hashtags searchable and clickable on its platform. Over the years, social media sites learned to rely on this symbol to catalog their enormous bulk of the content, and they would not advise you to post content without one.

Hashtags in the context of business advertisements work both ways. It spares the users from searching for content they would like to watch, and the business people are happy because there are fewer chances of being overlooked. Brands reach those viewers interested in the product and are searching for them on the digital platform.

Hashtags must match the content shown, and they should narrate everything about the particular idea.

For instance, #Snoozzzapalooza, by mattress maker Simmons, was an attempt by the company to rope in young customers. Their challenge was facile: dive into your bed. People responded gladly from the confines of their bedrooms. More than 1.1 million TikTokers participated in shooting a video on Tiktok about how they jumped down on their beds. In their earnest attempt to join in the challenge, the TikTokers made #Snoozzzapalooza famous (*TikTok For Business, 2021*).

For Simmons, it meant brand awareness among people likely to buy their products. Once a brand is famous, people want to possess its product. There is nothing wrong with wanting to make a moment memorable. And what best way to remember a challenge than buying a souvenir from the brand?

Businesses get noticed in the digital marketplace when they use an identification mark. A hashtag is an example of it.

Hashtags give businesses a form, a standpoint, and sometimes the status of an aspirational role model. That is why you should choose hashtags with deliberation.

Sometimes brands use hashtags to drive social consciousness. They participate in trending social debates on workplace harassment and sexual abuse.

#MeToo moved many brands to create awareness about women's rights and protection. In India, Durex, the condom brand, Ajio, e-commerce owned by Reliance Retail, #Askingforit by an advertising agency Ogilvy and Mather, and many others spread consciousness on maintaining women's protection in the workplace and domestic environments.

But some brands misstepped on hashtags. Australian fashion brand Kholo went widely off the mark when as an introduction to its #MeToo collection, it mentioned "the whole #MeToo thing," which immediately met with repercussions from social media users across the world. The galling thing was naming some of the products from the couture "Sex on Legs" and "Take Me Off Slip Dress."

The leaders of the movement were not amused. Kholo had to apologize unconditionally and rename the collection "The Magnificent Women Collection." But the damage was done (*Marketing in the #MeToo Era, 2018*).

In essence, hashtags help brands to cultivate an image. They can utilize it to build a communication bridge and inspire a feeling of oneness with society.

You get the best business advertising deal by using hashtags on social media sites—they are for free. Whatever you want to tag, you will likely find a hashtag for that. But before you type ABCD after a hashtag, you must find if there is a page for it to land. The keyword you type must be accurate.

If you are naming the page, you must select the right keywords. You can do it by using # before any keywords or phrases suitable for your business. For example, let your page be #MyEfforts.

You create a page naming it #MyEfforts and place the information on it that you want to share with your audience. What you put should be relevant and accurate because this is what your audience will know about you and your business.

Types of Hashtags

Hashtags can be Brand & Campaign Hashtags, Content Hashtags, Trending and other different hashtags used for varied reasons.

Brand & campaign hashtags promote brand marketing. Content hashtags tag anything, from favorite or promoted products to trips to a location. Trending Hashtags are on topics that are up for grabs. If you are fortunate to find a trend developing around your content, you should engage in the discussion. The more you engage positively with the users, the more favorable their response is.

Brand hashtagging is the act of using the brand's name as the keyword to popularize the brand, like #JustDoIt. Chat hashtags tag a text from the discussion topic urging interested people to join in the discussion.

During NBA championships, #NBAtalks became a popular spot for the audience to chat. The team with the largest fan base had an opportunity to interact with the supporters using the hashtag to get a healthy dose of encouragement.

Content Reflecting Tagging cast a view on the content; for instance, #MyPlate is the current nutrition guide for US citizens and is published by the USDA's Center for Nutrition Policy and Promotion. Other examples of this type of tagging are #EatFresh, #socialdistancing, etc. These are more used for public awareness programs.

Call To Action Tagging, on the other hand, encourage the audience to engage in some specific actions actively. In context to brand advertisements, they may drive your audience to visit your online store and utilize your services.

Using Hashtags Cleverly

Hashtags help you engage in active conversation, bring more information, and generate leads for your business. You can select good hashtags by researching the popular ones used by social media users and zeroing on the ones related to your brand. Probe into the hashtags to find out the more attractive and memorable ones.

Now, you are ready to make a hashtag for your brand. You can reach the target audience through this hashtag and socially interact with them. You can network and communicate at the same time through hashtags. More networking brings better prospects for clients' engagement with your business. Shopping may have gone virtual, but the social media pages still allow you to respond to your customer' queries and build trust. Hashtagging your content brings you closer to your potential customers.

Effective consumer interaction reflects increased brand visibility on social networking sites. However, hashtags should conform to the standards of the app's requirements; each social media platform supports hashtags differently.

Like all other online activities, Hashtags can be and should be tracked. Hashtag.org, Hashtagify,me, Ritetag, Topsy, etc., are some of the tools used to track the performance of hashtags. You must use a relevant tool for the site hosting your hashtag campaign or challenge. Topsy is a tool that tells you the influencers of a particular hashtag (*Vedantam, 2017*).

Hashtags And TikTok

TikTok hashtags label the video content that is uploaded on its platform for more effortless viewer engagement. If you are looking for content on gaming, for instance, #Gaming on TikTok will help you arrive immediately on thousands of topics related to gaming.

If you type in #PTD, you can happily watch content on the popular song by the Bangtan Boys, a South Korean Boy Band, Permission to Dance. The hashtag adds to the discoverability of the content, just like any other platform.

TikTok is an entertainment platform; its hashtags have a flavor of fun and recreation. Content in this category gets the maximum number of views, close to 535 billion. The next popular category is dance videos which receive 181 billion hashtag views. Other popular categories among TikTok's users are humor, tricks, fitness and health, home renovations and DIY, beauty, and makeup.

You may not opt to go for a full-fledged hashtag campaign, which is costly, but you should use hashtags on TikTok to improve the chances of getting your product discovered and build a fan following for your content. Let us understand in what ways TikTok hashtags can help you and why you should be using them.

Hashtags are simple techniques to generate leads for your business. A painless use of even a general #DIY can make your content *visible* to all those interested in DIY crafts. You can always guide the audience through a hashtag to your landing page.

Better visibility means better *engagement*. People liking or commenting on your posts increase engagement rates.

If you want to build a community for your brand, you may consider using a branded TikTok hashtag. You can use these hashtags to invite your audience and encourage them to create videos using brand-specific hashtags. There are many instances of such branded hashtag communities on TikTok; # BuxomBabe is one such community of influencers, beauty buffs, and the brand Buxom Cosmetics.

Branded hashtags are also the best ways to build brand visibility; if you have the resources, this is probably the best way you can invite and engage the audience to make content on your branded hashtagged campaign or challenge. You can also seek for influencer collaboration to have the desired results.

Chase Bank's #ShowMeYourWork challenge asked new graduates to flaunt their graduation walk. Many people participated in the challenge including Kevin Hunt.

On Tiktok, you can use hashtags that are specific to your industry. You would be able to locate other brands in your sector, identify your competitors, and unravel their methods. Learning the strategies used by others gives you an edge in business; on TikTok, you gain it as a complimentary service from the app.

You can search for ideas relevant to your products or services. TikTok's brilliant algorithm will show you the best possible ones in your area of interest. They are educational because you get ideas and learn specific strategies to improve your performance.

TikTok is a haven for influencers. They have millions of followers, and if you use their talents, they will showcase their expertise for your purpose and bring their followers to your site.

TikTok is high on presenting new ideas and content to its viewers; hence the searching experience is always trending. Do some work to locate a trending topic on TikTok and create hashtag content for it. As a bonus for your work, you get a chance to appear on the Discovery page to be viewed by millions of TikTokers worldwide.

TikTok tools such as Hashtag Expert helps you to keep a tab on the latest trending hashtags you may use for your content.

If a hashtag is extremely popular, people are interested in it. But how to find out which hashtags will give you the best results on TikTok? To get an idea, look for the content with the top view. You can also research which trending hashtags in your niche or industry get the most views. If you use them cleverly for your content, you get 'discovered' by the right audience at the right time.

The TikTok Discover tab marks some hashtags as significant, like #tiktokholidays, #whattimetobealive, #nativefamily, #competitivegaming, □Then Leave (feat, Queendom Come),□Hood Baby, etc. you can check the 'listicles' that put together the top hashtags in different categories. A tool like 'TikTok Hashtags' helps you locate the most liked ones concerning a certain theme. This particular tool estimates the number of posts on the hashtags, number of views, and post views.

The best practices to use hashtags on TikTok are to ensure the hashtags you choose should apply to the content, campaign, or the challenge. TikTok advises you to use a few handpicked hashtags that are readily shareable and instantly noticeable; too many of them can lose track.

Hashtags should be easy to spell and interesting but not controversial. You may use the same techniques for TikTok hashtags. You can also refer to your hashtags for other social media sites to understand what stimulates audience participation.

TikTok advises you to combine niche hashtags with the popular or trending ones to get the best effects for your campaign or challenge. Niche hashtags attract users already liking your content. They are less competitive; hence your post gets more chances of getting discovered.

A popular or trending hashtag can have outstanding exposure, but many people use them. Hence, the chance of getting discovered by them is challenging for a newcomer. For instance, #ForYou,

#ForYouPage, and #FYP are extremely popular to the effect they enjoy a combined view of some trillions. Many aspirants use these hashtags thinking that it would help them to become visible on the For You page. But the concept lacks evidence. Conversely, they are not the best crutch to rely on.

When you combine a popular or a trending hashtag and a niche hashtag, you can become popular among a well-defined audience. Use a niche hashtag and then combine it with #FYP or #ForYou to experiment.

An example of this is #Echohack and #FoodWasteTip with the trending #TikTokHolidays hashtag.

TikTok allows up to 300 characters in the caption, including the hashtag. It would be a good idea to make your captions short so that you have space for the hashtags. For the same reason, you should limit the number of hashtags you use. Select three to five best possible ones.

There is always scope for improvement, and TikTok wants you to find success on its platform; for instance, you may use TikTok analytics to search for opportunities to improve (*Zote, 2022*).

When the outlook of an app is so positive, it is no surprise that you evolve on the app.

Chapter Summary

- Hashtags are symbols that make your content visible on social media sites.
- Hashtags invite action from the users of the site.
- Brands use hashtags to create brand awareness.
- TikTok hashtags are viewed by billions of TikTokers worldwide.

In the next chapter, we will discuss trends on TikTok.

CHAPTER 8
USING TRENDS ON TIKTOK

The internet and the world wide web have marked the beginning of an epoch: The Age of Digital Communities. With social media platforms forming a central hub of interaction, digital communities extended their roots far and wide, crossing oceans and continents. The netizens of the world united under the folds of these communities to share their worldviews, concerns, moments of joy, happy reunions, and driving the latest trends in the world of entertainment and social matters.

The impact of these digital communities in all walks of socio-economic and geopolitical controversies can hardly be ignored. Service providers are now answerable to those they cater to, and they have to depend on popular trends and demands to satisfy the populace.

Starting from business houses to authors, everyone is riding on the back of current trends.

WHAT ARE TRENDS IN DIGITAL MARKETING?

Billions of people interact daily on social media sites on various issues like books, home decor, education, flowers and plants, astronomical events, political crises, witches, DIYs, and exotic recipes. They form groups, and groups grow into communities. Recently, Twitter has added a new feature: Communities! They described it as a "dedicated place to connect, share, and get closer to the discussions [people] care about most."

According to Maggie Lower, CMO, Hootsuite, thriving communities on social media sites are advantageous to the small businesses that no longer need to create a 'niche community.' They could just explore one that suits their business, join it, and worm into it. The point is, that if the business people are there for the consumers, the consumers will be there for them.

A timely example will demonstrate how trends help in business.

During the lockdown, BiGDUG received a flow of inquiries on home renovation. Although their niche area was the slow-paced B2B service sector, they considered aiming for more 'trending' DIY community on TikTok.

The company accessed the TikTok Creator marketplace to locate the favorite home improvement creator @theP001guy. BiGDUG sent him their products to use, and he should post videos while using them.

BiGDUG and @theP001guy, aka Miles Laflin, formed a long-lasting partnership. The company received millions of views and many impressions (*Social Media Trends*, 2022).

A business can hope to build a community of hungry consumers around its brand, but the dream may remain unrealizable if one does not adopt the proper strategies to succeed.

What Are TikTok Trends?

On TikTok, people create entertainment videos or watch them. If they like a video and get inspired, they may make their version of the theme. When many people join the activity, making it a movement that continues for some duration, the content can become a trend and dominate all the social media sites. The trends are typically entertaining and light-hearted.

An influencer can rapidly create a trend, more so when they are famous and popular. Once the trend reaches viral proportions, a user keeps seeing the trend popping up in a new avatar made by other users. The trend is so infectious that even a skeptical person joins in.

An influencer mainly initiates a trend on TikTok. These influencers joined TikTok and grew up with the app, literally learning about it and its people on the app itself.

They are a bunch of homegrown young boys and girls who make people marvel at their tricks and shows. Over time, they interacted with the followers, never letting them assume that the influencers were celebrities living in ivory towers. Conversely, they belong to the mass of people they bring their performance to, and a strong bond of love and trust exists between the influencers and their followers.

Influencers like Addison Rae and Charlie D'amelio are extremely popular, their followers numbering approximately a hundred million each. But TikTok is also a fertile ground to locate more consequential micro-influencers belonging to niche market places where they dominate the audience craze.

These micro-influencers have a fan following ranging from 1000 followers to 100,000 followers. They are the experts on their niche topic and can influence decision makings of their followers. You may have heard of Alina Gavrilov; she is a popular micro-influencer belonging to the fashion industry. People like Alina set trends in their areas of expertise.

You have to watch a TikTok trend to really understand what it is all about. Take, for instance, #fancylike by Applebee. It partnered with Walker Hayes, the country music singer, to name-drop in his song, "Fany Like," Applebee as the spot for a date night. The song names the menu too: Bourbon Street Steak and an Oreo milkshake. The campaign had a dance challenge choreographed by Haye's teenage daughter.

The restaurant chain showed TikTok fans dancing to the melodious tune in its advertisements. The challenge became a trend, receiving over 745 million views on TikTok (*Wheless, 2021*).

When you go through more TikTok trends, you will find that they are song-action-based videos that are very easy to manipulate to create your version and transform them into your story. You need to follow the trends to understand what piques the current audience's curiosity and interest (*Endler, 2021*). It would be aimless to try creating a trend of masking up when the pandemic is on the wane.

Evan Horowitz, CEO Movers+Shakers, and the creative genius behind the most viral campaign in TikTok history made for the e.l.f. Cosmetics stated, "I'd say over half, maybe the vast majority, of TikTok content follows a trend." Horowitz believes TikTok trends are "memes 2.0," and must be utilized if you are to spread your brand's awareness among the consumers.

Trends are "community-wide conversations" on TikTok; people actively express themselves by participating in the trends. Brands have the opportunity to engage with their consumers "organically" through trends.

To blend with the crowd yet make an impression on the viewer's minds, brands need to fully understand the nuances of a TikTok trend. Horowitz noted that when the users scroll through the content and the brand video appears, they must get pleasantly surprised and be able to appreciate the innovativeness and the fun factor in the ad. It must seek 'relevance' to the trend.

TikTok gives you the option of choosing the language for the text. Hence, if you want to make a video for your European customers, you can select the language they speak.

What's Hot Right Now?

Trends don't last long on TikTok. Its maxim is presenting new happening content to its users, so the one thing they can vouch for is Tiktok's entertaining capability. Thus, what is intense and exciting today can become outdated tomorrow. Rapper Kreepa used the soundtrack of a popular song, "Remember" by George "Shadow' Morton, to create his song "Oh No," which went viral quickly on TikTok. It started a trend which was participated by Tilly Ramsay, the daughter of famous chef Gordon Ramsay showing her pulling a piece of mischief on her father in the song sequence.

Approximately 20 million videos sprang up using the song. Then one day, all of it was suddenly gone.

The trends can become unpleasant and even offensive. If you accidentally jump onto an untimely trend, you may make yourself available at the receiving end of public disregard at best and an outcry or contempt at the worst.

Before we plunge into the slippery territory of what's hot now on TikTok (there are chances that it won't be by the time this book is published), let us understand what a trend on the platform is.

TikTok trends can be music, song, dance, hashtag, or challenge. Trends are born, and they die on the app every minute, sometimes so fast that it is difficult to keep track of them. Even how you brush your teeth can become a trend. If people like the way you brush your teeth, they will soon be making hundreds of thousands of videos on your post. In return, you get the credit for being a trendsetter. You may lay claim to a spot on TikTok's Hall of Fame.

Brands leverage this magical explosion of publicity and ride on it.

Let us look at some of the 'hot trends' on TikTok in 2021.

According to the app, they were on 'whipped coffee' and a fast and easy skincare routine. The trends in niche communities included Witchtok with 20 billion views and ArtTikTok or TikTokArt with 11 billion views (*Hirose, 2021*).

You may ask if there is any difference between a brand trend or a generally created one. There are no differences, and the brand advertisers often use trends made by TikTok creators.

You may fear getting lost in the crowd. You may also be scared by the sheer magnitude of mass hysteria and would instead think twice before becoming an active participant in it. You must realize that trends evolve. It is this inherent nature of changeability that we see in everything around us getting reflected in public behavior. There is nothing uncertain about it. Indeed, trends may resurface again at some other point in time.

You should take advantage of a trend; it is the easiest and the most cost-effective way to reach the masses. That was the idea of advertising: getting as much exposure as possible and then jumping onto the next trend, slightly tweaking it to suit your brand's sentiment. When you participate in people's movements, you inadvertently become a part of them. What else can be better to interact positively with your audience?

On TikTok, the app's algorithm rewards those who join trends. Their content gets more exposure than when they decide to stay put. When you scroll through TikTok's pages, you can see that the trends are distinctly apparent, and each video on them differs from the other. In other words, TikTok trends are fascinating.

According to a Hootsuite report on Digital Trends in 2022, the average time internet users aged between 16 years-64 years spend on social media sites is 2 hours and 27 minutes. That TikTok ads are more delightful than ads on other social media sites was noted in a survey conducted by Kantar.

21 percent of the participants in the survey mentioned that TikTok ads were more trendsetting, and businesses can benefit from them by actively participating in the trends. When your ads fit into your content and affirm the temperament of the trend, you can think about a way to entertain your audience without making them wary about being manipulated. That is the principle of advertisement in today's digital marketing.

Advertisements should be fun and engaging and not overbearingly promotional. Once you catch audience sentiment, you ride on the wave of popularity.

In 2022, the most meaningful trends on TikTok are as follows.

Dance And Song

Most dance videos on TikTok are amateurish and cute. TikTokers love dance movement, and you don't have to be a pro to dance for them. You just need to let yourself go and be the spontaneous you, pirouetting some fun-filled, easy movements to the beat of a lively band.

If you find a dance trend suitable for your business, you should consider utilizing it to create a short, entertaining ad for your brand. The app will tell you the trending dances. However, you may explore #dancechallenge, #dancetrend, or #trending dance to find one.

If you can find a suitable trend, you can tap on the sound to determine how TikTokers used it to produce different videos. You may also get a tutorial on creating a video or a meme on the trend.

In the sounds category, using a popular sound, be it song or music, and wrapping it cleverly around your storytelling is a way to utilize a trend successfully. During the pandemic months, TikTokers smiled at the picture of a pet dog with its paws neatly placed on a laptop's touchpad, looking sideways at the camera. The caption of the video read, "I just have a cold." To prove it, the dog made a coughing sound.

This theme sparked off video making using the original coughing sound. Many took the opportunity to acknowledge worldwide hysteria of someone coughing during the pandemic years (*Jaudon, 2022*). It takes great courage to make light of a grave situation, but that is perhaps the indomitable spirit of TikTok.

TikTok Mashups

You can add more than one song to a video. The technique used is called a mashup, where you layer two or more songs on top of each other or apply a transition between them to make a whole new song. The significant thing in mashups is the song, and many of these posts using #tiktokmashup2022 are *audio-only*. The images have an overlay of texts which mention the songs used.

Comic And Wit

One of the ways to make content interesting and eye-catching is to tart it up, and with TikTok, the young crowd loves content that is sharply witty, bold, and feisty. The gist is your content should not be heavy. Post something that tallies with the spirit of youthfulness.

Glow-ups

Glow-ups stimulate audience curiosity. In a typical glow-up, you post a few photos of yourself how you had been before and then how you gradually transformed into the current version of a more poised or glamorous self. The wait-for-it factor plays well with audience engagement.

Glow-ups can be on any topic, like your business's history, a transformation of a cluttered workplace to an organized one, etc.

Magical Transitions

You don't need a specialized degree to edit your work on TikTok. There are many ways to make seamless transitions within the videos; you can toss your camera, lose focus, zoom in, and pan out. You can deftly use TikTok's in-app editing tools to make simple or complex changes in your video shooting so that the effects merge seamlessly to create magical camera work.

A good camera work enthralls viewers, making them go over it more than once.

You can even reverse TikTok videos and play them backward. For this, you may use the time section in the effects menu of the app's video editor to locate the Reverse menu. You can see a preview of your video before uploading it on the platform. If you don't like it, you may remove it by selecting None.

Reversing a video can help in spawning fresh content related to the idea.

You can also apply other effects like Repeat, which loops your video, or Slow-mo, which sets your video in slow motion.

Get Yourself Vulnerable

Getting vulnerable is not insulting to your self-worth. Contrarily, it shows the human side of your nature. It removes the taint of being a superhuman or one devoid of all emotions. TikTokers appreciate honesty, and they understand the support you may need to boost your business. The app has a special place to honor vulnerability. After all, it deals with the most vulnerable period of human life: youth.

It may not be exactly a trend, but an honest approach can generate goodwill and support. TikTokers believe in the expression of emotions and not bottling them.

You may Ask Other Content Makers To Join In To Leave Comments

TikTok is an active platform; you can utilize this spirit by urging others to make the comments come alive. For instance, You may ask them to develop clever video titles. The thing you want most is audience participation with your content. Keeping this goal clear in your mind, you can think up numerous strategies to power your content.

Include Your Family

It is another way to make authentic content. Family members and their close association with you and your work make your efforts look genuine. Indeed, there are many family trends on TikTok, like the Lily Modern Family Blooper.

TikTokers are primarily young and finding a member of the older generation among them participating in making entertaining videos often has a redeeming effect.

Pop Culture

TikTok is full of trending ideas that originated from a raging television series or movie. A song from In the Heights happened to be the tune of voice for many TikTokers. A two-lined dialogue from Big Mouth became the 'sound' for more than 90,000 videos; the popular television series Squid Game sparked off bologna-making tutorials, musical mashups, and innumerable tracksuits. People love the craze. You may enjoy watching how TikTokers created innovative content from Squid Game.

'A-day-in-life'

You may think your life is boring, but just find out how many TikTokers love and comment on your video on a day of your life. Invite them to walk with you as you leave for your work, get frustrated, interact with colleagues, enjoy a break, come home to a super-happy pet, and mess up your dinner—all with a smile in the setting of hip hop music and sound.

Reply With A New One

Why reply to your comments in a text when you can create a new video on it? You can use the art of calligraphy to respond or make a video showing the effectiveness of your product or how to use it. Waterproof sneaker brand Vessi used their creative talent to show that their sneakers were machine washable as a reply to a query from a user.

Culinary Art

There are certain modes of engagement that never grow old or get boring. Cooking and baking are areas where people always show their interest.

Satisfying Videos

TikTok and other social media sites are now the hubs for showcasing satisfying videos. These videos are easy to watch, relate to repetitive movements, sometimes in slow motion and have a calming effect on the mind. They have become a part of psychological therapy.

Oddly Satisfying videos can include domino shows, parlor tricks, soap cutting, glitter slime, mixing of sand or paint, and even cleaning a stove in repetitive acts. Contrary to the after-effects of frantic internet use on electronic devices, anything that induces sleep is a satisfying video.

Niche Content Creation

Cleaning a stove was not just a simple, satisfying video; it was the start of 'cleantok,' an app dedicated to, you guessed right, cleaning. Some other examples of niche communities are gymtok, planttok, dadtok, etc. Each of them is a treasure trove of ideas on which you can base your theme of content creation.

It is easy to explore for yourself such a niche community. Just type a word and attach tok to it. But the best way for you to arrive at your community on TikTok is to scroll through its For You page, like the videos you are interested in, and comment on them.

TikTok's algorithm will do the rest of the job by catering to videos in your niche area of interest. Once you locate the people you want to build a relationship with, post content they will like and interact upon. You should also actively participate, energizing your audience, encouraging them, and piquing their interests.

TikTok For Business asserted that niche communities or 'subcultures' on the app are far more lasting than the trends. On such platforms, people exchange ideas that are distinct from the mainstream. Diverse topics are up for discussion, from a zombie apocalypse to anime.

The subcultures have their own code of ethics, style, and form. You have to get acquainted with it before you post your content. In #CraftTok, for instance, it is usual to see e-girls lip-synching to music as they apply makeup adeptly; in the same tempo, you can also find paper-makers kneading paper pulps.

Subcultures are the source of identity, a spot for aggregating like-minded people with similar interests. If you are to contribute to the subcommunity culture on TikTok, you must remember its mantras: entertainment, and creativity. To this, you may add TikTok's flavor of authenticity, where you can express how you genuinely feel about something. Your audience will also retain the same temperament while interacting with you.

The trends in niche communities are often the harbingers of bigger trends like #CottageCore. The challenge went viral in 2020, followed by an upsurge of billowing white dresses.

Backstage Stories

Behind-the-scene videos are educative and expressive. They describe the stories of your business that the audience cares for. Logan's Candies, a California-based confectionery company, gathered half a million followers after posting how they make their sweets.

Strong Brand

Nothing beats a strong brand. It's about having a consistent and identifiable face for your business.

Brands stand for honesty, quality, and efficacy. You give good after-sales services, address complaints, and prompt responses to queries related to your brand.

Although it forms the core of the company's success, the brand does not become strong by itself. Company strategy, time, and a continuous effort help build a brand strong. People identify you by your brand. If you can build one, it by itself will be a trend.

Leveraging Trends For Business

Businesses choose TikTok for marketing because of the app's magnitude of organic reach. Its simplistically demonstrative videos have the strangest tendency to become viral. Probably the trends show how users of social media sites are looking for an escapade from the mundane. In their efforts to dodge the plain vanilla, they morph it enigmatically to create content for TikTok.

If you want to promote your business on TikTok, you don't require the support of a million followers or a viral trend. What you need instead is the audience appropriate for your business. On other social media sites like Instagram, Facebook, and Twitter, the chance of getting visibility is less. Even if they do, the period of exposure is a matter of a few hours. With TikTok, the situation is much better than this. It declared that content on it has a shelf life of 90 days. You can indeed find videos on the For You Page that runs for months because they are still getting engagements.

TikTok is a mine of sub-communities or niche communities. Everyone can locate one to their taste.

Since the app boasts of the huge number of trends that germinated on it, you should leverage them for your business. You can express your brand identity, engage with the users cheerfully, and gain an advantage from the whole experience.

What is a trend on TikTok? It's a trope based on music and dance in a short video format. Each user puts their impression on it. Therefore, the theme, although common, does not really get old. It keeps morphing, appearing in further embodiments. Perhaps you would have been charged with plagiarism on another platform, but on TikTok, it is experimentation on an idea.

So, don't take yourself too seriously; no one else does, not at least on TikTok.

You should locate a trend that suits your niche area of the community. An example of a trend is #leanback by @wavewyld. You pose for the camera, look up, and lip-synch the lyrics to join the trend. In the text, mention some problems you are currently facing. Lean back, drop a punchline in the text stating how you cracked the issue or didn't get discouraged by it.

This trend can relate to a vast number of business niches. Think about how you can use it in matters concerning health, diet, hair care, makeup, fashion, jewelry, and other subjects. Anyone who is the influencers, content creators, boutique owners, dietitians, and artists can join the trend by sharing their creative sides.

TikTok does not make a compilation of the trends. It presents the users with a collection of popular and more usual videos depending on the users' activities on the app. If a video is a new trend, it shows an alert. When you make a video on such a trend, try to add a jaw-dropping effect and keep it within your subcommunity to get the best possible exposure.

Trends are usually on current events that have gained public attention. It can be an event like the Super Bowl or the recent forest fires. Lots of people would be discussing it. When you locate a hot topic, ascertain if it fits your business. Your brand, goal, and vision should correspond to the outlook of the trend. Nothing is as appalling as jumping on a mismatched trend.

Where can you find them? Try the Discover page of TikTok. The app updates all its trends here. You can find a variety of trends like hashtags, sound effects, and branded trends promoted by businesses. The app notifies the number of videos made on each of the trends.

However, when a trend shows up on the Discover page, it has already gained momentum, and in all probabilities, it would last for a few days more. Maybe, people are tired of seeing multiple versions of the same trend and are thirsty for new ones. The obvious punchline and the predictable ending take away the charm of watching them. Still, it would be unwise to neglect them. They can give you exposure to the TikTok audience, who in turn will come to know you.

How do you know which ones are upcoming trends and good to work on? Because they are fresh, these trends will last for nearly a week on TikTok. If you happen to make a video on a new trend, chances are that not many people have seen it. It is the right one to select for your business promotion. Since it is something new, people will watch it to the end. Keep the video short and add a strong CTA to your content to arouse people's interest.

When you have only a TikTok account for a specific purpose like a small business, your exposure to variety becomes limited. It will be challenging to identify trends with a fewer number of engagements. Therefore, you need to widen your search horizon. The trick is to open a second empty TikTok account besides your small business one.

You need not engage with anything on this second account, which you will solely use to scroll the For You page. You will see more variation here than in your original account. Scrolling rapidly, you can feel the repeating patterns of audio, video, and texts in the contents. Look for things that are engaging and different from the rest. If you hear a new song or see a lip-synching video that promises an outline for a theme, tap on the sound logo at the bottom of the video.

You will arrive at a page showing how many users have made a video using the sound. You can even see the videos ranked by popularity and the publishing date. Do not select themes that are more than a week old or have had more than 100,000 videos already made on them. You may select a theme that has recently produced a few thousand videos—indicating increasing popularity. It should be a new trend, maybe a few days old.

You can take a snapshot of the page showing the video and track it for popularity which often burgeons overnight on TikTok.

Let's consider that you have found a theme in its prime. The next step would be to adjust it to fit into your niche and represent your brand faithfully. As you work on it, you must make it your story. Most creative things are on some preexisting idea or plot. Copying an idea or a piece of music is not necessarily an error, but following in toto is. That would make the user unimaginative and the audience discontented. A successful imprint is less of a copy.

For instance, in one of the trends on the theme song, "I'm bad" by Michael Jackson, the content makers gave a sharp twist to the usual theme of making a "Jackson move" in black-and-white. They flaunted center stage and on the hood of a car and posed with swords, standing on tiptoes, leaning and twisting their bodies back at an angle in an effortless movement of being lifted in the air (Stelzner & Wyld, 2021).

Indeed, a song and dance sequence video can tell more stories than a mere text. In TikTok, you get the advantage of all three, video, audio, and text. The length of the video depends on the song's duration. The theme song for the trend, The Fresh Prince of Bel-Air, lasted 14 seconds. A video this long may need a bit of an effort to make. You can make an album of photos to give you a ready supply of clips that you may stitch together to create a video in a shorter time.

TikTok believes in giving you multiple chances. If your first-time venture did not do well, don't lose heart; some people try many times before producing one successful video.

What will you do with the videos that did not perform? Let them be, and don't try to delete them because the app's algorithm may not respond well to deleting contents. It may assume that you don't identify with your content. You must own the responsibility for your content as your creation.

Although you don't need to jump on every trend, be sure to participate in one that suits your business profile. The reasons for unsuccessful attempts can be participating in a trend too late, not making the trend a personal story, and not editing it well. You must follow all the requirements, for instance, if it requires special effects, you must use it skillfully.

Chapter Summary

- TikTok trends are themes on song and music depicting actions that are innovatively eye-catching.
- Trends on TikTok are great for business leverage.
- Identify TikTok trends which can be helpful for your business.

In the next chapter, I will guide you to get started on TikTok.

CHAPTER 9
A GUIDE TO GET YOU STARTED

In 2020, TikToker @aly.sherb posted a video about a woman who kept a McDonald's hamburger and fries in a box in her closet for twenty-four years. The food items were in their original packaging that mentioned the date. What surprised her and all the viewers was that the food items were still just the same after twenty-four years. The bread was intact and not molded, the meat uniformly brown and round. The fries she took out from the paper bag looked as if they were made fresh.

Another incident occurred close to the one stated. This was in Utah; David Whipple claimed to own the world's oldest hamburger from McDonald's, which would be soon nearing its drinking age. Like the older woman's burger, the burger that sat with him for twenty years looked fresh.

The web world was brimming with blog posts, articles, stories, videos, and memes. As the videos went viral and more and more people came up with similar content, purists, nutritionists, and even ordinary people were concerned. What was McDonald's feeding generations of people?

McDonald's chose to respond to the younger person's complaint. Its response was a blunder. Barbara Schmiett, the then PR with

McDonald's Utah, commented, "In the right environment, our burgers, like most other foods, could decompose." Her official response bore the title, "Response To Myth That McDonald's Burgers Do Not Decompose."

CONSUMERS ARE NOT FOOLS

Everyone knows what McDonald's or, for that matter, any fast food is. People don't eat them to stay healthy; they are the cheat foods that keep minds silenced and satisfied if we don't consider the after-effects of guilt and shame.

But the food that should mummify, mold, smell bad, swarm with larvae in various stages of pupal development, or even crumble to pieces and do not is of genuine concern. What are we eating then? Pieces of tanned leather?

Study McDonald's reply. It reeks of condescension. What did the fast-food chain mean by 'Right Environment' and 'Could'? 'Shouldn't' *right* food go rotten? McDonald's was challenging our concept of food.

Besides, the fast-food giant wasn't even sure if its food could rot in the right environment.

It went further ahead in its explanation, and not surprisingly, it started lecturing. The statement clarified the *right* environment: sufficient moisture, without which bacteria and mold may not grow. Water, either in the food or surroundings, *could* cause the decomposition of their burgers.

Schmiett instanced the case with homemade foods, where decomposition would not occur without moisture. But McDonald's is not home-made food, and all home-made foods rot, change color, texture, and form over time.

Schmiett added that McDonald's makes burgers from 100 percent USDA-inspected beef almost as an afterthought. She said they don't add preservatives or fillers; the only things present are a "touch of salt and pepper."

But the damage was already done.

McDonald survived because it was a giant corporation with worldwide networks. But that may not happen with small or medium business owners. Modern business owners must learn to respect consumer demands, outlooks, queries, and concerns. McDonald's case was a learning lesson on the emotional intelligence of any individual related to business (*Bariso, 2020*).

With the advent of social media platforms, users know where they can go, immediately expressing their concerns and grievances. Videos like McDonald's can become viral within a minute's notice. It can make or break a brand's reputation.

Businesses in the digital marketplace should accommodate the importance of consumer forums. They must learn to respond with feelings, and on platforms like TikTok, one can use the power of audio-visual storytelling to interact with the audience. A backstage story of how they source their raw products, prepare food, and how fresh and juicy their burgers look would have shown the humanistic face of McDonald's.

The Digital Age

We live in a digital age, and many of the older generations had to relearn the mannerisms of social media sites and acquire new technological skills to avoid the feeling of "social alienation." Nobody wanted to be left behind. Those skeptical about digital presence had made a beeline for it long back.

Leading marketing consultant Brian Honigman said that 55 percent of Americans on social media sites are 45-54 years old; the baby boomers (1946-1964) are a new demographic on social sites. Their inclusion on these platforms means increased traffic and the development of social sites as a marketing arena. It shows how fast individuals adapt to newer modes of communication and marketing technologies (*Cohen, 2016*).

Businesses nowadays are no more suspicious of digital platforms, and they don't consider social media interactions a challenge or an uphill task to perform.

Indeed, a callous professional attitude by businesses has churned out new forms of protests as social media boycotts. In 2020, Indian digital payment platform brand PhonePe faced one such netizen outcry against featuring celebrities like Aamir Khan and Alia Bhatt's association with the app.

Social media boycott is the latest *trend* discussing topics from patriotism to discrimination and favoritism. What does this mean for you if you are to open an online business? Online presence is not a fanciful idea; it has become necessary for survival. More and more people are looking *at* the web-based internet for any purpose rather than looking *up* the billboards advertising brands or services.

Social media allows consumers to express themselves and business people to respond to their customers on their pages. As a business owner, you cannot ignore the importance of social media forums where you get feedback for your business. Your customers interact with one another on social media platforms to spread the news about your business, good or bad. You need to learn the language of social media responses.

Andrew Pearson, VP of Marketing at Windsor Circle, a Predictive Marketing platform that establishes a contact between the retailers and their customers to help make repeat sales, said organic social media is one of the most vital channels for marketing and communication. The online survey that he used as a reference mentioned that 87 percent of responders used this mode of communication. In the future, this number could only grow.

The digital marketplace is also informative. Where else do you learn how your business is performing vis-a-vis your competitors'? Your competitor's business is thriving online, and yours is not implying that you need to rethink your social media marketing strategies.

You have to utilize these sites to arouse consumer awareness of your products and interest. But you have to be careful that you do not seem overly keen on selling your products.

To avoid such feelings among your audience, you may prepare videos on various topics regarding your business. While some can showcase your products, others can tell the audience how to use them, how you make them, what difference they would make when used, and the offers for the early birds.

A sequential story-telling can retain and stoke audience curiosity. You should take advantage of that. Using this method, you spread awareness and be versatile in reminding the audience about your products.

You can also show how to use your products for something unusual. For example, we all know the traditional use of a cup or mug. But how about using it to poach eggs?

You may try breaking an egg into the cup and then slowly sliding it into simmering water over the stove. You can surely make a video on this, the audience would marvel at the concept, and you can highlight your product with a catchy message like the way to make perfectly poached eggs is super-easy with your brand of cups.

The use of hashtags and keywords helps you locate your customers; once they show interest, you can guide them to your online store. You have to remain alert to interactions and consider them before you respond. Placing yourself in the position of a curious and sometimes disgruntled customer may help. It is your chance to get social, albeit from a safe distance.

Businesses must communicate with customers to enhance the brand's impression. When you interact, customers believe that you are interested in them, friendly, receptive, and reachable. Each one of these criteria builds brand reputation and maintains it.

After all, you have to measure the cost-benefit ratio for your business. Social media sites offer you convenient and efficient exposure to a wide range of audiences. You can even access online Data-Based Services (DBA). These remote services reduce IT expenditure, making your business better managed at a lesser cost of operation. You can respond effectively to the various needs of your clientele.

Most of the transactions, mainly the B2C types, are carried on smartphones. You must ensure that your website or social media strategy is compatible with smartphones and can give a rewarding shopping experience (*Wicks, 2015*).

Here are some metrics regarding the significance of the social media marketplace and why every B2B and B2C business should be on it.

Scott Stratten, the creator of UnMarketing, commented on how people spend more internet minutes on social media sites like Facebook and Instagram. He also noted a shift in video making from YouTube to other social sites for communication. Accordingly, users would better access sites like Facebook and TikTok for brands and video monetization.

Heidi Cohen, marketing strategist and bestselling author of "Marketing Rebellion" and "Cumulative Advantage," is a Chief Content Officer at Actionable Marketing Guide. She thinks that the social media marketplace is still evolving.

It is a good place to build brand awareness, increase audience numbers, generate leads, and promote sales. However, its role as a marketing tool to assess the achievement of business goals is still not clear. She suggested using CTA to obtain measurable proof of the marketing impact of social media. She also stressed increased budget allocation to help improve the digital marketplace.

While it is true that social media marketing needs further up-gradation and refinement, like the inclusion of the sales team into the social marketing efforts, such improvements can only happen as a course of development. As more and more brands and businesses become visible on the digital marketplace, it evolves further, which is natural.

If you are present in the digital marketplace with your business, you will be a participant in the process of evolution. There can be no other way to grow.

TikTok Is The Watch Word

Let us take a moment to reflect upon TikTok's mission statement or its purpose for being. It says, "to capture and present the world's creativity, knowledge, and precious life moments, directly from the mobile phone." TikTok believes that everyone can be a creator and emboldens users to share their creative zeal and style through their videos. TikTokers can be themselves when they express their imaginations. Hence, the content on TikTok can be unpolished and unsophisticated. But they are genuine and natural.

Probably people were tired of masquerade, so rife in the current cultural milieu; perhaps they wanted to be themselves for a while. Whatever the reason, after initial trepidation, people responded well to TikTok. Soon, people released their bottled-up emotions and took to the stage to perform.

Users did not reject these eccentric performances. Contrarily, they voted in favor and jumped on the bandwagon to produce offbeat videos— the wackier, the better. Whether this is a new trend of cultural evolution is difficult to say, and perhaps it is not the time yet; TikTokers went on merrily guiding and goading the showbiz on social media sites.

Anyone can become a content creator on TikTok. The app, as a mentor, provides all assistance, including free tools to enhance the video. It acquired in two years the number of active years, which took six years for Instagram to accomplish.

Companies like NFL and Universal ran their ads on TikTok, and TurboTax used the platform during tax collection periods. The companies used specific hashtags, dance-based challenges, pop-up ads, or simply in-feed ads. One thing they made sure about was using the app to reach people.

For those who still doubt the impact of TikTok on the business industry, it will suffice to say that it has paved the way for faster content creation and customizing for audience satisfaction. The proof, of course, is in the pudding itself.

If TikTok hadn't been effective, other giant social media sites like Instagram would not have added features similar to TikTok. In 2020, Instagram beta tested a new story display on their platform; one could easily move and choose between stories that caught up with the regular feeds. Users of the platform showed keen interest in narrating and sharing their accounts on the platform (*Encaoua, 2020*).

Brands get attracted to a place where people swarm busily. Facebook updated its Facebook marketplace and made costly additions to improve users' experience. The acquisition of GIPHY alone cost Facebook $400 million.

The app Zynn has monetized user experience; any user can earn points, later redeemable as gift vouchers or cash, by simply watching the content and interacting with others on them. Is Zynn a threat to TikTok as the latter had been to Facebook and Instagram, inducing them to make noteworthy changes?

The Digital 2022 Global Overview Report presented mind-blowing data on the popularity of TikTok. Although the data mining site could not provide year-on-year change on TikTok, they mentioned an impressive quarter-on-quarter growth on TikTok's own tools, which showed an increase of TikTok ad reach by 7.3 percent in three months starting October 2021. The ads reached 885 million people worldwide, not including those below 18 years of age.

During this period of 90 days, the app added more than 650,000 new users on average, coming to eight new users every second (*TikTok-Advertising Audience Overview, Jan 2022*).

TikTok's tools report ad-reach data for a selected number of countries, which means that data from many are not present in its report. These data also do not include a large group of TikTokers aged between 13years-17 years or data from Douyin. India and Pakistan have banned the app, which means a sizable global population doesn't appear in these stats.

Globally, TikTokers spend the same time using the android app as global Facebook users. But whereas the time spent on TikTok increased by 48 percent, time spent on Facebook has remained static over 2021.

In a survey by an investment firm Cowen that appeared on the Business Insider in January 2021, TikTok is the "top app" for making young people, mostly aged between 13 years- 34 years, aware of your brand.

The survey mentioned the app is performing well in brand publication responses compared to apps like Facebook and Instagram regarding the stated age group. How important are publication responses?

The top brand publishers are Red Bull, Adobe, GE, Equinox, SAP, Acorns, and Moz. Software tools like WordPress and YouTube have reduced the cost of the social media business, making it easy for all businesses to enter the digital marketplace to build a wide-based, trusted follower base that they could monetize.

Brand publishers strategize to drive revenue to their main products or services while projecting them as content publishers. The businesses sponsor blogs, infographics, webinars, presentations, videos, podcasts, interactive visualizations, PDFs, social media content, newsletters, and other means to interact with people. It is one of the best methods to engage your audience.

When you consider brand publishing, you become the author, editor, and publisher to establish your brand identity. Think about the different ways of narrating a story and how to embellish it with a doodle, a cartoon sketch, or a SlideShare presentation to highlight the brand's key features. You have to concentrate on the quality of your content. Selling the products right away is not your goal. It will happen eventually.

On TikTok, you can create your brand's story.

You must also respond fast and meaningfully to complaints and negative reviews. After an initial negative response, a happy customer can potentially become a faithful client.

On social sites, people wanted faster responses. 52 percent of the customers expected a response from the brand within a week of giving an online review, particularly if the review was negative or critical. 53 wanted a response within an hour; on Twitter, 72 percent wanted a quick response to a negative comment (*Campbell, 2016*).

Business owners can track their response times to determine how well they are addressing customer issues.

TikTok's earnest desire to improve the app experience means only more significant growth for the android app in 2022 (*Kemp, 2022*).

A Glimpse Into The Earnings of Known TikTokers

YouTube and Facebook share a portion of revenue from advertisements with their influencers. However, TikTok does not directly apportion its profits with the influencers. Instead, it builds a Creator Fund, a monetization tool using which the viewers can pay their favorite influencers. The influencer must have had 100,000 views on their videos over 30 days or have at least 10,000 followers.

Personal Finance influencer Preston Seo, with 2.1 million followers, mentioned earning $1,664 from the Creator Fund between January 2021 and May 2021. His TikTok account makes between $9-$38 per day.

Influencers get "virtual gifts" by live-streaming their content on TikTok over and above what they earn from the Creator Fund. According to influencer Lucy Davis, each program can fetch between $20-$300.

Preston Seo also earns on the app through affiliate revenue and sponsorships. He charges around $600 per sponsored post on TikTok. Another influencer, Atlanta Clarke, charges between $350-$600 per sponsored post.

Deanna Giulietti, a lifestyle influencer, fought against an adverse situation of job loss during the Covid-19 pandemic. She calls herself a 'hype girl' to illustrate her positive frame of mind and indomitable spirit. She experimented with the apps TikTok and Instagram, making videos of her day-to-day activities, flaunting her favorite dresses, and chronicling her preparations for different events.

She used several funny phrases like "it's a 10/10" or "peep the shoe," and her audience came to associate these phrases with her. Her spirit and self-affirmation won her 1.6 million fans on TikTok (*Melendez, 2021*). Giulietti earned more than $500,000 from brand partnerships on Tiktok and Instagram in 2021.

TikTok influencers often collaborate to work together. They make TikTok houses, and the HoneyHouse in Los Angeles is one such premise. It constitutes eight influencers from the millennial generation, who collaborated on health, nutrition, happiness, and fitness.

They released a 17-page media kit method they discussed on Business Insider. They used the ways to get brand sponsorships.

Promoting songs is one of the top ways to earn money on TikTok. Music marketers and record labels collaborate with Tiktok influencers to make a new track popular. Nicole, Natalie, and Nika Taylor, the triad of TikTok influencers with over 10 million followers, mentioned that they charge $750 for a single video content making, $1400 for two, and $2000 for three videos.

For micro-influencers with fewer followers, the charge may vary between $20-4150 per content, according to Austin Georgas, who spend some time working with music marketing. Tiktok music marketers are hiring micro-influencers over superstars for their organic reach, lesser expenses, and capabilities to produce more intimate and soulful experiences for the audience.

In 2021, the TikTok account "Hydraulic Press Channel" uploaded a video showing a stack of money "crushed" out of existence. As anticipated, the account "CEO of crushing" built a massive fan base of over 11 million followers. Music marketers decided to host creators making hydraulic post videos and DIY slime posts to host their song releases on Tiktok (*Whateley, 2022*). A new journey of video monetization began.

Useful Tips to Get Your Business Started

You should use the current trends on TikTok. They can be hashtags or memes that you can modify for your business purpose. TikTokers track down content using trending hashtags, and using them will display your content to a large audience.

You would not be the only person to use TikTok to gain popularity. It serves both your purposes when you get to express your creativity and gain viewership by adding some twists that you know the audience will love watching on an already popular theme. Kraft used the hashtag #KraftMacMeSkip to get over 6 million views.

Your ad should appear instructive, educational, inspiring, and entertaining, but not too promotional. Brands use TikTok mainly to promote and spread brand awareness. You can make subsequent posts to promote your brand engagingly once you have built up a fan base on the app.

You should not hesitate to engage content creators or influencers on TikTok. They would know how to engage the viewers meaningfully. And if you choose them wisely, they will be the ones that understand your business perspectives and the techniques necessary to display them skillfully to the audience.

TikTok has a creator Marketplace where you can locate content creators. Influencers can describe the products, offer promotions, and give the links to your online store to the consumers. If you engage influencers, they will tell their followers to use your products because they have used them and liked them.

A 9:16 video format makes the video a piece of captivating work. It means that your content appears on the entire screen alongside the messages. Use various backgrounds and surroundings to give your content a colorful and thematic angle. On TikTok, you are free to create shifting sceneries, variable camera angles, project spur-of-the-moment decisions, zoom in on your camera, and black-outs; indeed, the possibilities to get unique content are endless.

Some of the most aesthetic and visually stunning pictures are taken using very few palettes. You can highlight some colors and tone down others. Instead of focusing on the subject, you can focus away to accentuate details we normally ignore.

You must have a Call to Action within the content. It means you are action-oriented and do not shy away from demanding some results. The audience also understands what they need to do following the video.

TikTok's Ad Manager has features for clickable CTAs. Use them to get more traffic on your landing page, website, online store, or app store. CTAs increase conversions; you can even use them to offer future promotional content to the audience who engages with the CTAs.

Starbucks on TikTok gave the next course of action to the viewers in its New Year's campaign, #GoodVibeMessenger. Using CTAs imply that the audience should not just skim through videos and move on to the next ones dispassionately.

Caption your content to give it an identity. Viewers often watch TikTok without sound, like at work, waiting at the doctor's office, or for the metro. Captioning your content enables them to understand the message you deliver.

On TikTok, as on any other social media site, you must know the appropriate length of viewer attention span. Make it short and snappy, but if too short, the audience will be dissatisfied and maybe clueless; too long, and a viewer may even move away before you can display the essential element of your content.

TikTok metrics suggest an appropriate video length of 21-34 seconds is best for viewer engagement. Dan Slee, a digital communications expert, studied the best ten 100 TikTok videos in 2019 to find that 80 percent were less than 20 seconds long. The optimum duration, he said, is 15.6 seconds on TikTok.

Audience memory is short; the more you tap into it and engage with it, the better it is for your business goals. One way to never lose touch with your audience is to make batches of videos. Once you get enough views on the initial content, you should follow it up immediately with another one.

The viewers will not engage with all your content identically. They will ignore or reject some content. As you interact with them by posting more and more content, you will know what to create to engage the audience positively.

Audience engagement patterns do not vary much from one platform to another. If you are a newcomer to the platform, you may not get the best data to show when your audience's in-app behavior. If you have other social media presence, you can utilize them to know audience behavior patterns (*McCormick, 2022*).

When brands initiate their business journey on TikTok, they often post to try out varied content types. They collect feedback to ascertain which ones get the most engagement. Once they hit upon a formula, they repeat it to drive maximum engagement (*Zotara, 2022*).

TikTok's algorithm also prefers consistent posting. It does not appreciate when you keep your audience waiting. Hence, when you start on the app, post as many times as possible. TikTok recommends 1-4 posts per day.

But is there a best time to post your content on TikTok? One exists for most of the apps, and for TikTok, according to Influencer Marketing

Hub, the best time to post is Tuesday at 9 am. Thursday at midnight, and Friday at 5 am.

The exact times mentioned are as follows.

- Monday: 6 am, 10 am, 10 pm.
- Tuesday: 2 am, 4 am, *9 am.*
- Wednesday: 7 am, 8 am, 11 pm.
- Thursday: 9 am, *midnight,* 7 pm.
- Friday: *5 am,* 1 pm, 3 pm.
- Saturday: 11 am, 7 pm, 8 pm.
- Sunday: 7 am, 8 am, 4 pm.

The ones italicized are the best time for posting on TikTok.

What are the poor timings to post on TikTok? According to the Influencer Marketing Hub, they are 5 pm, 6 pm, and 9 pm on any day of the week; 10 am-3 pm on Sunday through Wednesday; midnight -4 am on Friday through Monday, and any time after 9 am on Tuesday. You can use these times to create more content that you can release appropriately.

Your posts gain momentum by the app's algorithm. Utilizing the best time slots gives you maximum organic reach for your posts by 118 percent on TikTok. Hence posting at the right time means more likes, shares, and comments.

However, if the best time to post is, for example, 3 pm on Friday, you should upload your video four to five hours before the peak hours to accumulate views and engagements. By the time it is 3 pm, your video has gained the right momentum.

You can have an unpaid Pro account on TikTok by tapping on the hamburger icon on your profile. Select Privacy and Settings and locate the Pro account to turn it on. It gives you an overview of video views, profile views, and follower numbers over the last 7-28 days.

A Pro account gives you updates on each of your content alongside some necessary insights. You can also gather some knowledge about your followers, gender, top activities, and peak time on the app.

Business analytics served on the desktop instead of getting them on the cellphone is always preferable. Go to your profile photo on the top right corner and click on "View Analytics." You may also watch a tutorial video by Brie Anderson on TikTok that shows you how to get your analytics on your desktop.

TikTok analytics can tell you who your audience is, and it may be enough to make calculated guesswork of their app-engagement patterns. TikTokers typically use the app many times a day, so if you miss one, you can make use of the others.

A social media management platform like Hootsuite can give you information on the best time to post for a social media site. You can also follow the accounts of other businesses in your category and find out their best hours to post content. While starting on the platform, you can follow their instances because they know the behaviors of your target audience.

What then are you waiting for?

Your content must be satisfactorily pleasing and stand apart from the rest. Jump on a trend, pick up a hashtag, make a meme, don't push yourself too hard, enjoy the game, and make your viewers enjoy it. Do not post shocking or offensive content.

A study by SEMrush found that humor is the best topic, with 58 percent of the viral videos being funny and merry. Surprise also works well with the audience, and 24 percent of viral videos had a surprise element. 51 percent of viral videos portrayed a person talking to the audience. Surprisingly, the study found that dance videos received views but not many shares or comments.

Chapter Summary

- Digital technology and social media platforms drive current socio-economic relationships.
- TikTok, because of its vast outreach, is a veritable mine for brand advertisements.
- The TikTok influencers market is lucrative.
- Start your business on TikTok with some valuable tips from TikTok For Business.

CHAPTER 10
PATIENCE AND DISCIPLINE WILL TAKE YOU PLACES

It's great to run a business, but business planning, execution, and keeping it alive takes time, patience, effort, and discipline. Without discipline, 90 percent of companies fail. Discipline and adherence give you an essential resource: mental grit.

It takes discipline to research the minute details of an endeavor before you launch a business; discipline enables you to patiently assess situations and test them instead of working on assumptions and making hasty decisions.

The areas of discipline for a successful business venture are as follows.

THE SEVEN SKILLS

Discipline is goal and result-oriented. Goal setting gives you a vision for your business. You need to fix your business goals one year from now and long term. The results your efforts show are indicators of the achievement of your goals. You should assess them regularly to measure progress, setbacks, the effectiveness of a method, and any re-orientation of ideas or techniques if required.

At least seven guiding techniques can give positive results when practiced consistently and methodically in business matters.

Discipline 1: Identify Your Customers

The goal is to market your business smart. You have to identify before starting a business who your ideal customers are. A target market comprises a group of people with common characteristics that you surmise will buy your products. They are a small component of your target market.

Determination of an ideal customer depends upon studying customer behavior and actions on social sites and the web. You should consider who can buy your product or service or are likely to buy them in enough amounts and at a price you may need to change to be in the business or start it.

Once your business progresses, you can feed customer details into a sturdy Customer Relationship Management (CRM) system. You may use your knowledge to decide your next course of action.

Discipline 2: Marketing Strategy: Lead Generation

What is your unique selling proposition, or USP? Is it your ability to talk through misunderstandings and solve differences? Or, do you understand customer mentality? For productivity, you must identify the strong points of your business and your USP. They give you a competitive edge over other businesses in your niche.

It can be about the benefits you can give to your customer or the feature of your products. Each business has its distinctive characteristics, and you must identify yours.

Your progress and activities must be recorded and assessed regularly.

Discipline 3: Developing A Sales System

You must formulate methods for how you can convert your leads into business. Also, customers should come back to you for repeat business and bring new clients. When that happens, it means growth for your business.

Customers want their money's worth in value and utility of products and services. Your business should appeal to them both logically and emotionally. It is the surefire way to lead the customers through all the five tiers of the sales funnel: awareness, interest, desire, action, and re-engagement.

The sales process should be measurable and consistently performed, and you should be able to repeat them.

Discipline 4: Be Proactive Rather Than Reactive

You being proactive means considering all the angles of a business carefully. You have to think about the more minor details and the broader outlook. For example, your office location, decor, and staff selection can be minor details. Broader implications are the feasibility of your venture concerning the current market scenario, longevity, effects on the environment, and other matters. You need to consider your business as a tree, its components, and the entire forest as part of an ecosystem.

When you do proactive thinking and formulate your strategies, you suffer less from sudden setbacks or accidents. You do not miss out on opportunities that will come your way. But you may miss them if you have not proactively prepared yourself to avail of them.

Discipline 5: What Is Your Most Important Goal?

Ask yourself and remind you of it every moment of your waking hours. It will keep you motivated in a venture. All ventures seem very exciting initially, but if you do not train yourself to focus on what you want, you will lose the sense of direction.

Instead of wasting time getting distracted in activities of little or no relevance to your business, you will need mental discipline to stay on track with things that matter. You may be busy, but it may not be sufficient to bring results unless your actions relate to your business goal.

While tools will help you monitor your business progress, you cannot allow a set of systems and tools to control all aspects of your venture. Business means dealing with people, and you must give it your personal touch.

If you are a company, good team leadership means a lot to the team members. You must be disciplined and focused on monitoring your team members' strengths and weaknesses. You should be able to guide them in their difficulties.

Discipline 6: Long-term Goal Setting

Any business takes time to develop. You can build customer relationships that will make your venture a long-term affair. Social media sites are the best places where you get to know your audience, their feelings, and their wants.

Discipline 7: Have Time For Yourself And Your Family

All areas of your life should manifest discipline, including your health and personal life. You must also have time and vitality for family reciprocities. Your business may lose a sizable chunk of value without a satisfying personal life.

When you are disciplined, you allot time for each of your activities like exercise, diet, chores, work, and other things of significance. You do not miss out on life.

Discipline does not mean rigid routines of self-punishment, which you must endure through gritted teeth. It means you enjoy the freedom of work and leisure time at your own pace. You gain experience, confidence, and resilience. All of which are formulas for success.

Chapter Summary

- Discipline is the key to success.
- It keeps you motivated in stressful times.
- It gives you self-trust, courage, and the method to succeed.
- Your customers and employees feel validated and satisfied knowing they are in good hands.

AFTERWORD

TikTok is a social media app that promotes short-from lip-synching videos featuring various ways of entertainment. Its users are young; they make the content, grow in popularity, and drive audience craze on the app.

TikTok's rise has been sharp and critical, particularly when the world reeled from a pandemic and its after-effects. It provided engagement and diversion and, in its wake, opened up opportunities for an alternate source of income for many who lost their jobs during the pandemic.

A remarkable increase in the app's popularity only helped more and more people find an avenue for expressing their diverse interests. Take the exciting story of a Texas-based Episcopalian priest and ex-marine, David Peters, based in Austin, who took to TikTok to make the church popular. Everyone enjoyed his quirky yet endearing video, where he used mash-ups to portray past and modern, holy and silly, in the same video format. The videos went viral.

It is the reason why your business should also be on TikTok. The ways you can reach out to your potential customers are inexhaustible.

This book attempted to provide you with the knowledge of what

TikTok is and why it is suitable for your business. Contrary to the claims, there is no proof that TikTok manipulates data. It is a business house and believes in maintaining integrity to "inspire creativity and bring joy."

Social shopping as a concept development was a natural step for TikTok because shopping is a natural phenomenon with the TikTokers. A TikTok survey in 2020 of its users found that the app inspired shopping by the users. #TikTokMadeMeBuyIt reached more than 6 billion views.

TikTok is no more a site for spreading brand awareness; it is where users make purchases. This trend will undoubtedly grow in the future. TikTok tested live-stream events with Walmart in 2021. The brand's exposure was boosted by seven times more than expected, and TikTok's following increased by 25 percent.

It announced an association with Shopify and Square. Consumers can directly shop on the app through a link on the brand's business profile.

Business houses like Manly Brands and Kylie Cosmetics signed up for the venture and saw growth.

Your business can tag its products in organic posts; the customer can buy them from the online storefront where the app will direct them.

E-commerce is the future for business, and TikTok is your business's e-storefront.

If you enjoyed reading this book, please do not forget to leave a review. Your views will make a difference.

REFERENCES

5 Features And Advantages Of TikTok For Digital Marketers. (2021). Ram.

7 Tips For Small Businesses to Hack The TikTok Algorithm. (n.d.). Https://Boosted.Lightricks.Com/7-Tips-for-Small-Businesses-to-Hack-the-Tiktok-Algorithm/.

10 Clear Reasons Why You Need Digital Marketing. (2018).

10 Compelling Reasons Why You Need Digital Marketing For Your Small Business. (n.d.). Https://Www.Maxeffectmarketing.Com/Why-Digital-Marketing-for-Small-Business.

A Brief History Of TikTok And Its Rise To Popularity. (2020, August 30). Big 3 Media.

A Guide to Hashtags on TikTok. (n.d.). Https://Boosted.-Lightricks.Com/a-Guide-to-Hashtags-on-Tiktok/.

Advantages of Small Business and the Economy. (n.d.). Https://Www.Verizon.Com/Business/Small-Business-Essentials/Resources/Advantages-of-Small-Business-and-the-Economy/.

Ahmed, A. (2021). *TikTok is the New Platform for Brands Who Want Their Products Reach the Ages of 13 till 35.* Https://Www.Digitalinformationworld.Com/2021/01/Tiktok-Is-New-Platform-for-Brands-Who.Html.

Alexander, L. (2022). *The Who, What, Why, & How of Digital Marketing*.

Balkhi, S. (2019). *How to Use TikTok to Promote Your Business*. Https://Www.Entrepreneur.Com/Article/340216.

Battisby, A. (2021). *An In-Depth Look at Marketing on TikTok*. Digital Marketing Institute.

Blunt, W. (2021). *7 TikTok Trends and Challenges Your Brand Can Use This Holiday Season*. Https://Www.Shortstack.Com/Blog/Tiktok-Trends/.

Bowman, C. (2022). *How Much Do TikTokers Make? Here's 7 of the Highest-Earning TikTokers*. Https://Www.Gobankingrates.-Com/Money/Entrepreneur/How-Much-Do-Tiktokers-Make/.

Brenner, M. (2018). *Why Social Media Is Important for Business Marketing*. Marketing Insider Group .

Bretous, M. (n.d.). *TikTok Trends B2B and B2C Marketers Should Watch in 2022*. Https://Blog.Hubspot.Com/Marketing/Tiktok-Trends.

Bump, P. (2021). *8 TikTok Marketing Examples to Inspire Your Brand in 2022*. Hubspot.

Business success is about discipline. (n.d.). Https://Onevision-Consulting.Com/Business-Success-Is-about-Discipline/.

Campbell, A. (2013). *What is a Hashtag? And What Do You Do With Hashtags?* Https://Smallbiztrends.Com/2013/08/What-Is-a-Hashtag.Html.

Chang-Soon, J. (2022). *How to Use TikTok Marketing for Business*. Https://Animoto.Com/Blog/Video-Marketing/Tiktok-for-Business-Guide.

Cherepakhin, I. (2021). *8 TikTok Power Features & Benefits for Digital Marketers*. Https://Www.Searchenginejournal.Com/Tiktok-Power-Features/416430/#close.

Choudhary, N., Gautam, C., & Arya, V. (2020). *Digital Marketing Challenge And Opportunity With Reference To Tiktok-A New Rising Social Media Platform.* INTERNATIONAL JOURNAL OF MULTIDISCIPLINARY EDUCATIONAL RESEARCH.

Cohen, J. (2016). *Social Media is Even More Important in our Modern Marketing Future.* Https://Blogs.Oracle.Com/Marketing-cloud/Post/Social-Media-Is-Even-More-Important-in-Our-Modern-Marketing-Future.

Collen, J. (2020, July 31). *Is TikTok Marketing Really The Future of the Digital Marketing Industry?* Socialnomics.

Dhariwal, P. (2020). *Discipline is key to success.* Https://Timesofindia.Indiatimes.Com/Readersblog/Consultantscounsellors/Discipline-Is-Key-to-Success-24805/.

D'Souza, D. (2021, July 22). *What Is TikTok?* Investopedia.

Elliott, J. (2022). *TikTok for Small Business: Tips from Business Creators.* Https://Www.Uschamber.Com/Co/Grow/Marketing/Small-Business-Tiktok-Tips.

Encaoua, D. (2020). *How Much Has TikTok Changed the Digital world?* Https://Www.Linkedin.Com/Pulse/How-Much-Has-Tiktok-Changed-Digital-World-Daniel-Encaoua/.

Endler, J. (2021). *Share on facebook Share on twitter Share on linkedin Share on pinterest Share on email What is a TikTok Trend?* Https://Media.Syft.La/What-Is-a-Tiktok-Trend/.

Foxwell, B. (2020). *15 Most Useful TikTok Marketing Tips in 2022.* Https://Esm2.Iconosquare.Com/Blog/15-Most-Useful-Tiktok-Marketing-Tips-in-2022.

Geyser, W. (2021a). *TikTok Marketing for Beginners – A Marketer's Guide to Advertising on Tiktok.* Influencer Marketing Hub.

Geyser, W. (2021b). *Tiktok Video Ad Specs and Best Practices for 2022.* Https://Influencermarketinghub.Com/Tiktok-Video-Ad-Specs/.

Geyser, W. (2021c). *Your Ultimate Guide to TikTok Hashtags.* Https://Influencermarketinghub.Com/Tiktok-Hashtags/.

Geyser, W. (2022, March 31). *What is TikTok? – Everything You Need to Know in 2022.* Influencer Marketing Hub.

Gymshark – A TikTok Influencer Marketing Case Study. (2020). Let's Influence.

Hait, A. (2021). *What is a Small Business?* Https://Www.Census.Gov/Library/Stories/2021/01/What-Is-a-Small-Business.Html.

Halpern, I. (2021, July 22). *Why You Should Be Using TikTok for Business in 2022.* Eternity Marketing .

Hamilton, F. (2019). *The power of hashtags in marketing: do they still work?* Https://Awario.Com/Blog/Hashtags-in-Marketing/#:~:Text=Hashtags%20help%20your%20-posts%20get,And%20engage%20with%20your%20post.

Hashtags Explained: The Complete Guide to Hashtags in Social Media. (n.d.). Https://Www.Takeflyte.Com/Blog/Hashtags-Explained.

Hayden, M. (2020). *How to use TikTok for Digital Marketing.* Eternity Marketing.

Henderson, G. (2020). *The Importance Of Social Media Marketing.* Https://Www.Digitalmarketing.Org/Blog/the-Importance-of-Social-Media-Marketing.

Herrman, J. (2019, March 10). *How TikTok Is Rewriting the World.* NY Times.

Hirose, A. (2021a). *14 of the Most Important TikTok Trends to Watch in 2022.* Https://Blog.Hootsuite.Com/Tiktok-Trends/#:~:Text=What%20is%20a%20TikTok%20trend,Trending%20TikTok%20video%20or%20theme.

Hirose, A. (2021b). *How to Create a Successful TikTok Marketing Strategy for 2022.* HootSuite.

How Chipotle Became The Most Followed Food Brand on TikTok. (n.d.). RightMetric.

How GymShark gained 3.4 million TikTok Followers 1 Success Story. (2022). House of Marketers.

How Gymshark Grew by 200%+ Year On Year and Hit £41M in Sales . (2019). Beeketing.

How Important is Self Discipline For Entrepreneurs. (2018). Https://Www.Entrepreneur.Com/Article/317270#:~:Text=Usually%2C%20self%2Ddiscipline%20provides%20inner,Reactions%20in%20a%20positive%20way.

How important is self-discipline in business success? (n.d.). Https://Www.Businessincorporationzone.Ae/Blog/How-Important-Is-Self-Discipline-in-Business-Success/.

How to Engage in TikTok Trends as a Small Business Owner. (2022). Https://Www.Shortstack.Com/Blog/How-to-Engage-in-Tiktok-Trends-as-a-Small-Business-Owner/.

How to integrate TIKTOK to your digital marketing campaign? (2022).

How to Use Hashtags on TikTok. (2021). Https://Www.Hashtag.Expert/Growth/Tiktok-Hashtags.

How To Use TikTok For Business In 2021 – Influencer Marketing Tips. (n.d.). Https://Theinfluencermarketingfactory.Com/How-to-Use-Tiktok-for-Business-in-2019-Influencer-Marketing-Tips/.

How to Use TikTok Marketing to Make Your Business Go Viral. (2021). https://www.youtube.com/watch?v=JRMSDbQtcoQ&ab_channel=LearnWithShopify.

How to Use TikTok to Boost Your Small Business. (2022). Https://Www.Hostpapa.in/Blog/Social-Media/Tik-Tok-for-Business/.

Hughes, D. (2019). *The Rapid Rise of TikTok.* Https://Digitalmarketinginstitute.Com/Blog/the-Rapid-Rise-of-Tiktok.

Hutchinson, A. (2021). *Pro Tips: TikTok Shares Advice on How Brands Can Establish a Presence on the Platform, and Generate Results.* Https://Www.Socialmediatoday.Com/News/pro-Tips-Tiktok-Shares-Advice-on-How-Brands-Can-Establish-a-Presence-on-Th/604626/.

Hysi, E. (2019). *10 Undeniable Reasons Why You Need Digital Marketing.* Https://Www.Linkedin.Com/Pulse/10-Undeniable-Reasons-Why-You-Need-Digital-Marketing-Elsa-Hysi-1c/? Trk=public_profile_article_view.

Jaudon, E. (2022). *TikTok trends: How to find them and make them your own.* Https://Www.Bazaarvoice.Com/Blog/Tiktok-Trends-How-To/.

Jerde, S. (2019). *The Washington Post Takes to TikTok to Drive New Subscribers.* Adweek.

Kelso, A. (2019). *Why Chipotle's Bet On TikTok Is Paying Off.* Forbes.

Kemp, S. (2022). *Digital 2022: TikTok Rapid Rise Continues.* Https://Datareportal.Com/Reports/Digital-2022-Tiktok-Headlines.

Key TikTok Trends For Businesses. (2022). Https://Www.Xanda.Net/Key-Tiktok-Trends-for-Businesses/.

Ku, D. (2021, November 8). *The Importance of Social Media Marketing in 2022.* Post Beyond.

Mahan, L. (2021). *Is TikTok the Future of Digital Marketing?* Inside Hook.

Maheshwari, D. (2022). *Why This is the Best Time to Use TikTok for Your Business?* Https://Www.Socialpilot.Co/Blog/Tiktok-for-Business.

Mariah, J. B. (2018). *How Important Are Small Businesses to Local Economies?* Https://Smallbusiness.Chron.Com/Important-Small-Businesses-Local-Economies-5251.Html.

Marr, B. (2022, November 1). *The Eight Biggest Business Trends in 2022.* Forbes.

May, T. (2021). *7 TikTok trends creatives need to know about.* Https://Www.Creativebloq.Com/Features/Tiktok-Trends.

McCormick, K. (2022). *The Best Time to Post on TikTok & How It (Surprisingly) Compares to Instagram.* Https://Www.Wordstream.-Com/Blog/Ws/2022/02/09/Best-Time-to-Post-on-Tiktok.

McGuire, A. (2021). *Chipotle TikTok Campaigns: How A Brand Uses TikTok Well.* Medium.

McLachlan, S. (2021). *The Best TikTok Hashtags to Use to Grow Your Views and Reach.* Https://Blog.Hootsuite.Com/Tiktok-Hashtags/#:~:Text=Hashtags%20are%20impor-tant%20to%20use,For%20You%20page%20(FYP).

McLachlan, S. (2022, April 6). *What is TikTok? Best Facts and Tips for 2022.* HootSuite.

McLachlan, S., & Newberry, C. (2021, June 29). *22 Benefits of Social Media for Business.* Hootsuite.

Medina, J. (2022). *5 Tips For a Killer Small Business TikTok Strategy.* Https://Www.Uschamber.Com/Co/Grow/Marketing/Small-Business-Tiktok-Strategy-Tips.

Miller, M. (2022). *40+ TikTok Stats Digital Marketers Need To Know.*

Mojica, K. (n.d.). Why Social Media is Important for Your Business Growth. *Digital Success.*

Monllos, K. (2022). *How small businesses are using TikTok to build brand awareness and boost sales.* Https://Digiday.Com/Marketing/How-Small-Businesses-Are-Using-Tiktok-to-Build-Brand-Awareness-and-Boost-Sales/.

Myers, L. (2021). *This Is How to Use TikTok Hashtags to Reach More People.* Https://Louisem.Com/378309/Tiktok-Hashtags.

Needle, F. (n.d.). *TikTok Ads Guide: How They Work + Cost and Review Process [+ Examples].* Https://Blog.Hubspot.Com/Mar-keting/Tiktok-for-Business.

O'Brien, C. (2022). *How to Use Hashtags Effectively on Social Media.* Https://Digitalmarketinginstitute.Com/Blog/How-to-Use-Hashtags-in-Social-Media.

Ocampos, J. (2020). *Why digital marketing is important for businesses?* . MM Matters.

Oracles, T. (2018). *11 Ways to Stay Motivated, According to Highly Successful Business People.* Https://Money.Com/Self-Discipline-Motivation-Tips-Successful-Business-Leaders/.

Parham, T. (2020). *How Small Businesses Can Leverage TikTok To Generate More Sales.* Https://Www.Sbdc.Uh.Edu/Sbdc/Small-Business-Tiktok.Asp

Patel, N. (2020). *8 Useful TikTok Marketing Tactics.*

Pellico, K. (2019). *How the Washington Post uses TikTok to engage with its audience.* CNN Business.

Perez, S. (2020, June 25). *TikTok launches TikTok For Business for marketers, takes on Snapchat with new AR ads.* Tech Crunch .

Pilon, A. (2020). *How to Use TikTok for Business.* Https://Small-biztrends.Com/2020/09/Tiktok-App-for-Business.Html.

Pittman, R. (2020). *How Chipotle Took Over TikTok.* QSR Magazine.

Pot, J. (2021). *7 TikTok marketing tips from small businesses.* Zapier.

Redhead, B. (2022). *What is the Impact of TikTok on Digital Marketing in Today's World?*

Reitere, S. (2021). *10 Brands That Rule on TikTok.* Social Bakers.

Ryan, O. (2021). *Hashtag Marketing: How to Use Hashtags for Better Marketing Campaigns.* Https://Mention.Com/En/Blog/Hashtag-Marketing-How-to-Use-Hashtags-for-Better-Marketing-Campaigns/.

Sadeh, G. (2021). *5 Great TikTok Hashtags Marketers Can Use for Massive Discoverability.* Https://Mention.Com/En/Blog/5-Tiktok-Hashtags-for-Massive-Discoverability/.

Sambol, A. (2019). *Digital Marketing In 2020 | 7 Reasons Why Small Businesses Need It.* Https://Blog.Marketo.Com/2020/01/Digital-Marketing-2020-Seven-Reasons-Why-All-Small-Businesses-Need.Html.

Schaffer, N. (2022). *5 Reasons Why TikTok Marketing Is The Hottest Social Media Trend For Businesses Today.*

Schwedel, H. (2018, October 4). *A Guide to TikTok for Anyone Who Isn't a Teen.* Slate.

Shah, K. (n.d.). *Importance of Digital Marketing in Today's World: 2022's Scenario.*

Sheikh, M. (2021). *How to use TikTok for business effectively and grow your audience.* Https://Sproutsocial.Com/Insights/Tiktok-for-Business/.

Simpson, J. (2020, July 23). *Why Your Business Should Be On TikTok (And Four Types Of Content To Promote Your Brand).* Forbes.

Smith, G. (2021, June 8). *The history of TikTok: From Musical.ly to the number 1 app in the world.*

Stelzner, M. (2021). *TikTok Trends: How to Leverage Trending Content for Business.* Https://Www.Socialmediaexaminer.Com/Tiktok-Trends-How-to-Leverage-Trending-Content-for-Business/.

Strapagiel, L. (2021). *8 Ideas to Get Your Small Business Started on TikTok.* Https://Www.Shopify.Com/Blog/Small-Business-Tiktok-Ideas.

Tay, L., & Teo, T. S. (2021, March 31). *The New Age Brand Strategy: Trends, Opportunities and Challenges.* Bird & Bird .

Taylor, N. (n.d.). *Why Are #Hashtags So Darn Important?* Https://Www.Naylor.Com/Associationadviser/Why-Are-Hashtags-Important/.

The Biggest TikTok Trends for Businesses to Use in 2022. (n.d.). Https://Blog.Wishpond.Com/Post/115675438359/Tiktok-Trends-for-Businesses.

The Changing Face of New Age Business. (2020, June 2). Pearl Academy.

Theisen, S. (2021). *5 Reasons Your Business Should Have A Digital Marketing Strategy.* Leighton Broadcasting.

Thomas, M. (2020). *A Quick Guide to Using TikTok For Business.* Https://Later.Com/Blog/Tiktok-for-Business/.

Three brands that nailed TikTok marketing. (2020). Media Update.

Tidy, J., & Galer, S. (2020, August 5). *TikTok: The story of a social media giant.* BBC News.

TikTok Business and Marketing Trends for 2021. (n.d.). Https://Boost-ed.Lightricks.Com/Tiktok-Business-and-Marketing-Trends-for-2021/.

Tiktok Earnings – Here Are Some of the Best Paid Tiktokers Today. (2021). Https://Academy.Wedio.Com/How-Much-Do-Tiktokers-Make/.

TikTok is the Future of Digital Marketing. (n.d.). Soidea.

TikTok Marketing in 2022: The A-Z Guide for Businesses. (2022). Https://Invideo.Io/Blog/Tiktok-Marketing-2021/.

Tillman, M. (2021, August 9). *What is TikTok and how does it work? Everything you need to know.* Pocket Lint.

Turvill, W. (2021). *Platform profile: A guide to TikTok for publishers (featuring 'Washington Post TikTok guy').* Press Gazette.

Valvano, G. (2019). *Digital Marketing Basics: The Importance of Hashtags.* Https://Www.Craftedny.Com/Importance-of-Hashtags/.

VAYNERCHUK, G. (2019). *WHY THE TIKTOK (FORMERLY MUSICAL.LY) APP IS SO IMPORTANT.*

Vedantam, S. (2017). *What is Hashtag Marketing? Hashtag Strategies to*

Engage Audiences. Https://Digitalready.Co/Blog/What-Is-Hashtag-Marketing-Hash-Tag-Strategies.

Want To Market On TikTok? 12 Top Tips For Businesses. (2022). Forbes Expert Panel: Https://Www.Forbes.Com/Sites/Forbesagencycouncil/2022/02/07/Want-to-Market-on-Tiktok-12-Top-Tips-for-Businesses/?Sh=53b54df6702d.

What is digital marketing? (2022).

What is Small Business? Types of Small Business. (n.d.).

What is TikTok for Business, and Why Does it Work? (n.d.). Growth Marketing Genie .

Whateley, D. (2022). *How much money TikTokers make, according to creators.* Https://Www.Businessinsider.in/Advertising/News/How-Much-Money-Tiktokers-Make-According-to-Creators/Articleshow/84078631.Cms.

Why are small businesses important for the economy? (2021). Https://Imm.Ac.Za/Why-Are-Small-Businesses-Important-for-the-Economy/.

Why Digital Marketing is Important for Small Business. (2021). Https://Digitalmarketinginstitute.Com/Blog/Why-Digital-Marketing-Is-Important-for-Small-Business.

Why Digital Marketing is Important for Small Businesses. (n.d.). Https://Www.Connectionmodel.Com/Blog/Why-Digital-Marketing-Is-Important-for-Small-Businesses.

Why is digital marketing important to your business? (2022).

Wicks, D. (2015). *Role of Social Media Marketing in Business.* Https://Www.Socialmediatoday.Com/Social-Business/Role-Social-Media-Marketing-Business

Widen, C. (n.d.-a). *8 Hacks for Small Businesses to Get Started on TikTok.* Https://Boosted.Lightricks.Com/8-Hacks-for-Small-Businesses-to-Get-Started-on-Tiktok/.

Widen, C. (n.d.-b). *How to Use TikTok for Business*. Https://Boosted.-Lightricks.Com/How-to-Use-Tiktok-for-Business/.

Widen, C. (2022). *41 TikTok Video Ideas For Small Businesses*. Https://Boosted.Lightricks.Com/41-Tiktok-Video-Ideas-for-Small-Businesses/.

Wooden, D. (n.d.). *7 Disciplines for Entrepreneurial Success*. Https://Www.Successwithcrm.Com/Blog/7-Disciplines-for-Entrepreneurial-Success.

Worb, J. (2022). *The Top TikTok Trends to Try This Week*. Https://Later.-Com/Blog/Tiktok-Trends/.

Zadeh, N. (n.d.). *TikTok Hashtags Strategy* . Sidewalk: https://www.y-outube.com/watch?v=OW1sRuqyoBs&ab_channel=SidewalkerDaily.

Zhu, X., Song, B., & Li, R. (2016). Business Trends in the Digital Era. *Springer*.

Zotara, J. J. (n.d.). *10 TikTok Marketing Tips & Best Practices*. Https://Www.Searchenginejournal.Com/Author/Jason-Zotara/.

Zote, J. (2022). *TikTok hashtags: how to use them to grow your reach*. Https://Sproutsocial.Com/Insights/Tiktok-Hashtags/.

www.ingramcontent.com/pod-product-compliance
Lightning Source LLC
LaVergne TN
LVHW051340050326
832903LV00031B/3653